ORACLE QUICK GUIDES
PART 3 - CODING IN ORACLE
SQL AND PL/SQL

Malcolm Coxall

Edited by Guy Caswell

Cornelio
Books

Published by M.Coxall - Cornelio Books
Copyright 2014 Malcolm Coxall
First Published in Spain, United Kingdom 2014
ISBN: 978-84-941783-7-5

"Space does not exist unless there are objects in it

Nor does time exist without events."

Contents

Preface and Audience

1. What are SQL, SQL*Plus and PL/SQL?
2. Basic Components of SQL
3. Basic SQL Language Syntax
    3.1 SQL Language Elements
    3.2 SQL Operators
    3.3 SQL Expressions
    3.4 SQL Functions
    3.5 SQL Clauses
    3.6 SQL Query syntax
    3.7 SQL Data Modification Language syntax (DML)
    3.8 SQL Data Definition Language syntax (DDL)
    3.9 SQL Data Command Language syntax (DCL)
    3.10 SQL Data Types in Oracle
4. Complex SQL constructs: Understanding Joins
5. Understanding Commit and Rollback
6. Basic architecture PL/SQLProcedures, Functions and Triggers
7. Basic PL/SQL Language syntax
8. PL/SQL Exception handling
9. SQL and PL/SQL: some standards for good coding appearance
10. Performance issues when coding in SQL
11. Installing and using a SQL*Plus client
12. SQL - PL/SQL Development Tools
13. Glossary of Terms

About the Author

Preface and Audience

Oracle Quick Guides: Welcome to Oracle Quick Guides, a series of quick learning guides for Oracle designers, developers and managers.

Guide Audience: These guides are designed to rapidly deliver key information about Oracle to the following audience groups:

> - Project Managers, Team Leaders and Testers who are new to Oracle and need rapid access to strategic information about the Oracle development environment.

> - Business Analysts, Designers and Software Developers who are new to Oracle and need to make a first step in gaining a detailed understanding of the design and development issues involved in Oracle.

Guide Contents: These guides have been divided by subject matter. They become increasingly complex and more specific the later the volume. Thus, part 1 is quite general but later volumes are quite technical and specific. Here in part 3, we introduce programming concepts and basic syntax for SQL and PL/SQL development, the languages most used in an Oracle environment.

All Oracle systems use SQL and PL/SQL in some part. Regardless of the user interface, system size or system process, at some point all Oracle systems use SQL in some way. Thus, knowledge of SQL is fundamental to an understanding of Oracle systems. We assume that the reader understands the concepts of relational database design outlined in Part 1 and Part 2 of the Oracle Quick Guides.

Our Objective: There are plenty of Oracle textbooks and user manuals on the market. Most of them are huge and only partly relevant to a particular group of readers. Therefore, we decided to divide the subject into smaller, more targeted volumes in order that you only get the information YOU need.

For example, a Project Manager doesn't need to know some of the more esoteric programming tips, but will need to know some of the strategic issues affecting design and testing. In a similar way, a Programmer is much more interested in the syntactic details of a piece of software than in the strategic issues affecting the choice of an Oracle upgrade path.

And so we have targeted these guides at particular groups with specific interests whilst trying to avoid overloading readers with too much detail or extraneous material.

Assumptions: We assume that the reader will be using Oracle 9i, 10g or 11g, although most of the material will apply equally to earlier versions of the Oracle RDBMS.

---oOo---

1. What are SQL, SQL*Plus and PL/SQL?

SQL stands for Structured Query Language. It is the language most used to communicate with a relational database.

According to ANSI (the American National Standards Institute), SQL is the standard language for relational database management systems. ANSI provides a standard for SQL, which is the basis for many commercial versions of the language.

SQL statements are used to perform fundamental database tasks, such as to enter and update data on a database, or retrieve data from a database. Some common relational database management systems that use SQL are: Oracle, SQL Server, Access, etc.

Is SQL standard? Yes and No. Although most database systems use SQL, most also have their own additional proprietary extensions that are usually only used on their systems. However, the (ANSI) standard SQL commands such as "Select", "Insert", "Update", "Delete", "Create", and "Drop" can be used to accomplish almost everything that one needs to do with a database. This means that SQL is very portable between database systems, even if you don't happen to be familiar with the local variant of SQL in a different database environment.

How to pronounce SQL? The first version of SQL was in fact called "Structured English Query Language" and had the acronym SEQUEL. Due to trademark violations on the acronym, the name was changed to Standard Query Language and abbreviated as SQL. So at first it was intended to be pronounced as "SEQUEL". Nowadays it's a matter of preference. The "cognoscenti" tend to call it SEQUEL.

A little history of SQL: SQL was initially developed at IBM by Chamberlin and Boyce during the early 1970s. This original version (initially called SEQUEL) was designed to manipulate and retrieve data stored in IBM's original quasi-relational database management system known as "System R".

In the late 1970s, Relational Software, Inc. (now Oracle Corporation) saw the potential of the concepts described by Codd, Chamberlin, and Boyce and decided to develop their own SQL-based RDBMS. In June 1979, Relational Software, Inc. introduced the first commercially available implementation of SQL, Oracle V2 (Version2) for VAX computers. Around the same time IBM continued their own development of what later became known as DB2 - their own proprietary relational database - also using SQL.

SQL became a standard of the American National Standards Institute (ANSI) in 1986, and of the International organization for Standards (ISO) in 1987. Since then, the standard has been enhanced several times with added features. But code is not completely portable among different database systems, which can lead to vendor lock-in. The different makers do not perfectly follow the standard, they add extensions, and the standard is sometimes ambiguous. On the other hand, differences in SQL implementations are quite obvious and manageable.

Why is SQL so important? These days SQL is ubiquitous. Although few end-users are aware of what drives most of their daily software systems, generally at the most fundamental level it is almost always SQL, which is the powerhouse of most commercial software applications in current use these days.

So, whenever there is a relational database involved (which is almost always), then the core software will eventually use SQL as the lowest level language for the retrieval and manipulation of data from the database. Whatever layers of software are built on top of a database, such as smart html web front ends, java, .NET etc., when it comes to interaction with the database it will be small tracts of SQL code that actually insert, extract and manipulate the data at the database level. SQL is the foundation of modern commercial software systems.

SQL and PL/SQL is used in all Oracle application software products. Oracle Forms and Reports, for example, both rely on SQL, as does Oracle APEX. Oracle Applications are based on software entirely dependent on SQL and PL/SQL. Even Oracle's own utility software systems like Enterprise Manager use SQL to interrogate the Oracle data dictionary.

Therefore, at a software engineering level, an understanding of SQL is immensely important to a fundamental understanding of the design and working of a lot of commonly used commercial software. It is therefore really worth putting an effort into acquiring a thorough understanding of the SQL language.

What is SQL*Plus? SQL*Plus is basically a working environment for a developer (or user) to create and execute SQL commands when using an Oracle database. SQL*Plus is the main interface to an Oracle Database server and it is packaged as a client with all Oracle software.

SQL*Plus provides an easy-to-use environment for querying, defining, and controlling data. Oracle, with SQL*Plus, has effectively upgraded SQL with its own SQL language extensions. SQL*Plus gives the developer access to these extensions and to the creation and execution of PL/SQL (see next section).

SQL*Plus is also a command line tool which is proprietary only to Oracle. A developer (or user) may access SQL*Plus via a client which can be installed on any client PC.

Who uses SQL*Plus? Despite the original ambitions to create a "query language for the common man", rarely do ordinary system users actually work with SQL or SQL*Plus directly. It isn't that friendly to a non-technical user and rarely are users willing to invest the time and energy in learning SQL.

SQL is a relatively simple query language for forming simple queries. However, it can become quite difficult for a user to master when anything other than very basic queries are required. In general, normal users are provided with some form of GUI tool or piece of software to interact with their databases, where they are able to use pre-defined SQL constructs to carry out their tasks, rather than giving them free access to SQL*Plus.

Technical users (like DBAs, developers and designers) will use SQL*Plus during development for prototyping queries and transactional code. But these days even developers tend to use the more friendly GUI based clients like TOAD or SQL Developer to interact with the database. Nonetheless, the command line SQL*Plus is still in constant use by DBAs and developers and is considered to be a fallback if all else fails or alternatives are unavailable.

What is PL/SQL? One of the problems with basic SQL is that it is not a procedural language. It is a super-efficient query language and data manipulation language and its entire set-based syntax is driven by these objectives. However, by itself, SQL cannot be safely used to build complex query or transaction processing software.

So, for example, if a query is executed in SQL and it retrieves zero records, the programmer may wish to branch to a new process based on this result. This concept is programmatically impossible in SQL, because the language simply doesn't contain the syntax for something like conditional testing or conditional branching.

SQL is totally "un-procedural". This means that it cannot detect or be made to branch due to any result or error state. Of course, this limits the language enormously, because even the simplest applications require some basic means of managing program control. SQL does not contain a concept of "If-then-else"

Of course, this fact is exactly what was intended by the original designers of the SQL language. It was never intended to replace the old 3GL procedural languages like C. Rather, SQL was intended only to provide an additional, easy-to-use, syntax layer to deal with relational databases.

Early methods of procedural processing with SQL: In the early days of development with Oracle the problem of a lack of procedural syntax in SQL was overcome by the creation of a suite of so-called "Pro" languages: Pro*C, Pro*Cobol etc. These 3rd generation software compilers offered the possibility of embedding and integrating SQL command tracts into 3rd generation program code. Thus, for example, it was possible to regain the full procedural functions of the C language whilst leveraging the superpower of SQL when dealing with an Oracle database. Pro*C is still in use today and is often considered to be a fast and efficient option for batch processing software.

Nonetheless, the introduction of a procedural version of SQL was always Oracle's objective and starting in 1988, the company launched PL/SQL which stands for Procedural Language/Structured Query Language (PL/SQL). PL/SQL is now Oracle Corporation's prime procedural extension language for SQL and the Oracle relational database. PL/SQL's general syntax resembles that of Ada or Pascal. It is a relatively easy language to master once the developer understands SQL.

PL/SQL is also one of three key programming languages embedded in the Oracle Database, along with SQL itself and Java. The introduction of PL/SQL meant that highly complex procedural software could now be built without the absolute need to use 3rd generation languages like C.

PL/SQL also opened up the possibility of storing software within the database itself and was part of Oracle's Object-Relational strategy of keeping software and data structures together in the same database.

---o0o---

2. Basic Components of SQL

SQL consists of several syntax component groups, each of which is used for a different purpose when working with a relational database:

- Query Language syntax for querying the database

- Data Manipulation Language (DML) for altering data in the database

- Data Definition Language (DDL) for defining data in the database

- Data Control Language (DCL) used to authorise users to access and manipulate data

We will now take a look at how these components are used in general, in both the creation and administration of an Oracle database and how they are used in querying and transaction processing.

Bear in mind that each of these components has its own large range of syntax and we will examine these in more detail later. For now, we provide simple examples just to illustrate these basic components:

2.1 Query Language syntax: This part of the SQL language deals only with extracting data from the database using the "SELECT...." syntax. SQL is especially good at extracting data based on complex set-based queries. A whole syntax is available to a programmer (or user) to construct very complex queries with a much abbreviated set of SQL query commands. A typical SQL query might read as follows:

```
SELECT     name,
           address,
           telno
FROM       employees
WHERE      name like 'KELLY%'
AND        termination_date is NOT NULL
```

Such a query seeks to find the employee details for someone with "KELLY" in their name, and who has also now left the company.

2.2 Data Manipulation Language (DML): Before data can be retrieved from a relational database, it must first be added to the database. The SQL language provides a complete set of transactional "data modification" syntax which is based on the following transactional concepts:

- INSERT: New data is added to a database table.

- UPDATE: Existing data is altered in a database table.

- DELETE: Existing data is deleted from a database table.

A typical DML statement might read as follows:

UPDATE employees

SET termination date = sysdate

WHERE employee_id = '4567712'

Such a statement would attempt to set the date of termination of an employee with the id 4567712 as today's date.

2.3 Data Definition Language (DDL): Of course before any of the above data query or transactional syntax can be used, a database also needs to be defined. The so-called metadata of a database is defined using syntax contained in the DDL part of SQL. Typical statements in DDL include "CREATE TABLE....", "CREATE INDEX" etc.

A typical example of a SQL DDL statement is as follows:

```
CREATE TABLE    employees
(employee_id     VARCHAR2(12) NOT NULL,
name            VARCHAR2(40) NOT NULL,
address         VARCHAR2(90) NOT NULL,
telno           VARCHAR2(15));
```

This SQL DDL is defining a table called EMPLOYEES which contains 4 columns, all of which can contain character data of a particular maximum length. The first 3 fields must have a value (this means a record cannot be inserted into the table unless these columns contain a value).

DDL is generally the exclusive domain of the DBA in an Oracle environment and special database privileges are required to execute DDL commands.

2.4 Data Control Language (DCL): In a multi-user database environment, security and privilege are everything. Obviously not every user can see or manipulate all data. Similarly, not every user can manipulate data in exactly the same way. Users have different needs and different rights of access to both data and what functions they are allowed to use.

In reality, a complex matrix of user privileges exists wherein users are granted access to certain database tables and certain data, and have certain rights to SELECT, INSERT, UPDATE and DELETE these data. In addition, there are a myriad of other privileges that are allocated to some users and not to others depending on their role in an organisation.

The control of these privileges is managed using the DCL component of SQL. The primary syntax of DCL is based on the following commands:

- GRANT (..... a privilege)
- REVOKE (.... a privilege)

For example, a user might be given access to a particular set of data as follows:

GRANT   SELECT,
            INSERT,
            UPDATE
ON   employees to scott;

In this example, the user called SCOTT is being granted the right to SELECT, INSERT and UPDATE data in the EMPLOYEES table.

DCL is the exclusive domain of a Database Administrator (DBA) in an Oracle environment.

---o0o---

3. Basic SQL Language Syntax

The following chapter is going to take a much closer look at SQL language syntax. We will divide this chapter according to the SQL components described in Chapter 2, but first we have to look at the rather more technical components of the SQL language elements themselves. This is essential to understanding what follows.

Obviously SQL is a very large (and growing) language, so we are going to confine the discussion of SQL syntax to the main statements that are in constant use in day-to-day commercial development.

Once defined, SQL extensions tend to remain completely stable. However, you should always refer to the latest Oracle user manuals for the version of SQL that you are working with to see the latest Oracle SQL extensions and the appropriate syntax for new extensions, if you are in any doubt.

3.1 SQL Language Elements:

The SQL language is subdivided into several language elements. These include the following:

- **Operators:** An operator is a word or a character used in a SQL statement WHERE clause to perform operations such as comparisons and arithmetic operations. Typical operators include =, >, IS, LIKE etc.

- **Expressions:** These can produce either scalar values or columns and rows of data. In the example above, we have the following clause:

    WHERE employee_id = '4567712'

    The expression here is '4567712'. The result of a SELECT statement containing this clause may be one or more rows of data.

- **Functions:** SQL includes a lot of built in functions which make queries easier to define and build. For example, the functions "COUNT", "MAX", "MIN" and many more mathematical and set functions are standard parts of ANSI SQL designed to make software development easier. These functions don't need to be defined again.

- **Clauses**: These are constituent components of statements and queries. (In some cases, these are optional.). For example, in the section above, the part of the statement:

    UPDATE employees

  is called a SQL clause.

- **Queries:** Queries retrieve data based on specific criteria. Queries are an important element in SQL. SQL started its life as a query language and this part of the language is certainly the most frequently used component of SQL in all software applications. Here is a simple example query selecting all columns and all rows from the table called EMP.

    SELECT *

    FROM emp;

- **Predicates:** These specify conditions that are evaluated to the so-called SQL "three-valued logic", i.e. a predicate is true/false/unknown. A predicate is also used to limit the effects of statements and queries, or to change program flow. In the same example above, the following is the predicate:

    WHERE employee_id = '4567712'

- **Statements:** This is the word used for a whole SQL sentence which may be used to affect schemas and data, or which may control transactions, program flow, connections, sessions, or privileges. The following is a complete SQL statement (ending in a semi-colon):

SELECT	name,
	address,
	telno
FROM	employees
WHERE	name like 'KELLY%'
AND	termination_date is NOT NULL;

- **Terminator:** SQL statements also include the semicolon (";") statement terminator. Though this is not required on every SQL platform, it is defined as a standard part of the SQL grammar.

- **Wildcards:** SQL uses several wildcards, most importantly '*' meaning all columns, and '%' for all values (except NULL).

We will now examine some of the more important and complicated of these language elements with some simple examples.

3.2 SQL Operators

An operator is a reserved word or a character used primarily in a SQL statement WHERE clause to perform operations such as comparisons and arithmetic operations.

Operators are used to specify conditions in an SQL statement and to serve as conjunctions for multiple conditions in a statement. The following types of operators exist:

- Arithmetic operators
- Comparison operators
- Logical operators
- Operators used to negate condition

Example:

```
SELECT      employee_id
FROM        wages_summary
WHERE       wage_amount + bonus-amount > 1000
```

In this example we are selecting the employees that have a sum of their wage and bonus payment greater than 1000.

Here there are 2 operators: The arithmetic operator "+" (addition) combining the wage and bonus amounts and the comparison operator ">" (greater than) comparing the amount with a fixed value 1000.

Let's take a look at these operators in a little detail:

3.2.1 SQL Arithmetic operators: The arithmetic operators are fairly obvious and are as follows:

- - Addition   +
- - Subtraction   -
- - Multiplication   *
- - Division   /

3.2.2 Comparison operators: These operators are used to make comparisons between 2 values or variables (operands):

=	Checks if the value of two operands are equal or not: if yes then condition becomes true.
!=	Checks if the value of two operands are equal or not: if values are not equal then condition becomes true.
<>	Checks if the value of two operands are equal or not: if values are not equal then condition becomes true.
>	Checks if the value of left operand is greater than the value of right operand, if yes then condition becomes true.
<	Checks if the value of left operand is less than the value of right operand, if yes then condition becomes true.
>=	Checks if the value of left operand is greater than or equal to the value of right operand, if yes then condition becomes true.
<=	Checks if the value of left operand is less than or equal to the value of right operand, if yes then condition becomes true.
!<	Checks if the value of left operand is not less than the value of right operand, if yes then condition becomes true.
!>	Checks if the value of left operand is not greater than the value of right operand, if yes then condition becomes true.

3.2.3 Logical operators: These operators are used to make logical comparisons:

ALL	The ALL operator is used to compare a value to all values in another value set.
AND	The AND operator allows the existence of multiple conditions in an SQL statement's WHERE clause.
ANY	The ANY operator is used to compare a value to any applicable value in the list according to the condition.
BETWEEN	The BETWEEN operator is used to search for values that are within a set of values, given the minimum value and the maximum value.
EXISTS	The EXISTS operator is used to search for the presence of a row in a specified table that meets certain criteria.
IN	The IN operator is used to compare a value to a list of literal values that have been specified.
LIKE	The LIKE operator is used to compare a value to similar values using wildcard operators.
OR	The OR operator is used to combine multiple conditions in an SQL statement's WHERE clause.
IS NULL	The NULL operator is used to compare a value with a NULL value.
UNIQUE	The UNIQUE operator searches every row of a specified table for uniqueness (no duplicates).

3.2.4 Operators used to negate condition:

NOT   The NOT operator reverses the meaning of the logical operator with which it is used, e.g. NOT EXISTS, NOT BETWEEN, NOT IN etc. This is a so-called "negate operator".

3.3 SQL Expressions: An expression is a combination of one or more values, operators, and SQL functions that evaluate to a value.

SQL expressions are like formulas and they are written in query language. You can also use them to query the database for a specific set of data.

For example, consider the basic syntax of the following SELECT statement:

```
SELECT      column1,
            column2,
            columnn
FROM        table_name
WHERE       [CONDITION|EXPRESSION];
```

There are 3 types of expression:

- Boolean Expressions
- Numeric Expressions
- Date Expressions

3.3.1 Boolean Expressions: SQL Boolean Expressions fetch the data on the basis of matching a single value.

An example of a Boolean expression would be as follows:

```
SELECT      *
FROM        customers
WHERE       sales = 10000;
```

In this example we retrieve all the columns (indicated by *) from the CUSTOMERS table, where the SALES column = 10000.

3.3.2 Numeric Expressions: This type of expression is used to perform any mathematical operation in any query, for example:

```
SELECT      count(*)
FROM        customers
WHERE       sales = 10000;
```

In this example we select the total count of records in the customers table (as a single value) where the customers have the SALES column = 10000.

3.3.3 Date Expressions: Date Expressions return date and time values or parts of them. For example:

```
SELECT      SYSDATE-30
FROM        dual;
```

In this query we find the current date-time minus 30 days.

3.4 SQL Functions: SQL has many built-in functions for performing calculations on data. These are extremely useful when SQL is involved in complex processing because this allow a developer to call highly reliable ready made functions rather than to have to code these functions from scratch.

The syntax of the functions varies slightly between implementations of SQL. Here we illustrate just a few useful Oracle function implementations. There are many types of function available in Oracle, divided into the following categories:

- Analytic / Aggregate
- Collection
- Conversion
- Date Time
- Data Mining
- Miscellaneous
- Model Clause
- Null Handling
- Numeric
- Object
- String
- XML

Oracle currently has over 300 pre-defined functions available. We won't repeat them all here and for a complete list of all the currently available SQL functions, you should consult the SQL documentation for the Oracle version you are working with.

3.4.1 A few examples of SQL Functions in use:

Analytic functions: Obvious examples of analytic functions include MAX, MIN and AVG. Here is an example of how they are used:

SELECT max(sales)

FROM customers;

This query returns the maximum sales value (a single value) from the CUSTOMERS table.

String Functions: A simple example of a string function trims off spaces from the right-hand side of a column in a table:

SELECT rtrim(employee_name)
FROM employees;

Numeric function: All the usual numeric functions are also available, like the SIN, COS, TAN, for example:

SELECT tan(incline_1)
FROM roof_dimensions;

3.5 SQL Clauses

Here is a basic SQL SELECT Statement syntax:

SQL SELECT Statement:

SELECT   column1,
column2,
column*n*
FROM   table_name;

And here are some examples of SQL Clauses that can be used in the statement:

SQL DISTINCT Clause:

SELECT	DISTINCT column1,
	column2,
	columnn
FROM	table_name;

SQL WHERE Clause:

SELECT	column1,
	column2,
	columnn
FROM	table_name
WHERE	CONDITION;

SQL AND/OR Clause:

SELECT	column1,
	column2,
	columnn
FROM	table_name
WHERE	CONDITION-1 {AND|OR} CONDITION-2;

SQL IN Clause:

SELECT	column1,
	column2,
	columnn
FROM	table_name
WHERE	column_name IN (val-1, val-2,...val-N);

SQL BETWEEN Clause:

SELECT	column1,
	column2,
	columnn
FROM	table_name
WHERE	column_name BETWEEN val-1 AND val-2;

SQL Like Clause:

SELECT	column1,
	column2,
	column*n*
FROM	table_name
WHERE	column_name LIKE { PATTERN };

SQL ORDER BY Clause:

SELECT	column1,
	column2,
	column*n*
FROM	table_name
WHERE	CONDITION
ORDER BY	column_name {ASC|DESC};

SQL GROUP BY Clause:

SELECT	SUM(column_name)
FROM	table_name
WHERE	CONDITION
GROUP BY	column_name;

SQL HAVING Clause:

SELECT	SUM(column_name)
FROM	table_name
WHERE	CONDITION
GROUP BY	column_name
HAVING	(arithematic function condition);

3.6 SQL Query syntax: The most common operation in SQL is the query, which is performed with the declarative SELECT statement. SELECT retrieves data from one or more tables, or expressions.

Standard SELECT statements have no persistent effects on the database (i.e. they don't alter anything). Therefore, in principle, executing a SELECT statement is generally a safe action. However, beware that a badly constructed SELECT statement against very large tables can cause huge computer resource demand.

3.6.1 Basic SQL Query construct: A query includes the SELECT keyword and a list of columns to be included in the final result immediately following the SELECT. An asterisk ("*") can also be used to specify that the query should return *all* columns from the queried tables. SELECT is the most complex statement in SQL, with a huge number of optional keywords and complex clauses that may include:

- **FROM:** The FROM clause indicates the table(s) from which data is to be retrieved. The FROM clause can include optional JOIN sub-clauses to specify the rules for joining tables.

- **WHERE:** The WHERE clause includes a comparison predicate which restricts the rows returned by the query. The WHERE clause eliminates all rows from the result set for which the comparison predicate does not evaluate to "True".

- **GROUP BY:** The GROUP BY clause is used to project rows that have common values into a smaller set of rows.

  GROUP BY is often used in conjunction with SQL aggregation functions or to eliminate duplicate rows from a result set. The WHERE clause is used before the GROUP BY clause. As a rule of thumb, in SQL, you "group by" every column *except* the column involved in the group set function. For example, here the group set function is SUM:

  ```
  SELECT       department,
               SUM(sales) as "Sales Total"
  FROM         order_details
  GROUP BY     department;
  ```

- **HAVING:** The HAVING clause includes a predicate used to filter rows resulting from the GROUP BY clause. Because it acts on the results of the GROUP BY clause, aggregation functions can be used in the HAVING clause predicate. Here is an example:

  ```
  SELECT       department,
               SUM(sales) as "Sales total"
  FROM         order_details
  GROUP BY     department
  HAVING       SUM(sales) > 1000;
  ```

- **ORDER BY:** The ORDER BY clause identifies which columns are used to sort the resulting data, and in which direction they should be sorted (options are ascending or descending). Without an ORDER BY clause, the order of rows returned by an SQL query is based on its chronological order of INSERT to the table: Here is an example of ORDER BY:

24

```
SELECT          supplier_city
FROM            suppliers
WHERE           supplier_name = 'IBM'
ORDER BY        supplier_city ASC;
```

3.6.2 Examples of SQL Queries: Take a look at the following examples to get an idea of the basic construction of a SELECT statement:

Example 1 (single table):

```
SELECT *
FROM products
WHERE price > 100
ORDER BY product_name;
```

This example query returns all columns and all rows from the PRODUCTS table when the value in the PRICE column contains a value greater than 100. The results are sorted in ascending order by the PRODUCT_NAME. The asterisk (*) in the select list indicates that all columns of the PRODUCTS table should be included in the result set.

Example 2 (two joined tables):

```
SELECT          suppliers.supplier_name as supplier,
                COUNT(product_id) as product_count
FROM            products,
                suppliers
WHERE           products.supplier_id = suppliers.supplier_id
GROUP BY        supplier.supplier_name;
```

This example demonstrates a query of multiple tables, grouping and aggregation by returning a list of suppliers and the number of products from each supplier. Note that the two tables are joined using the primary key of the SUPPLIERS table with the referential foreign key of the PRODUCTS table, which is the column called SUPPLIER_ID.

Example output might resemble the following:

supplier	product_count
ABC Supplies	4
Lovely Foods	298
Different vegetables	32
Jams of the world	102

3.6.3 Simple Sub-queries: Queries can be nested so that the results of one query can be used in another query via a relational operator or aggregation function. This nested query is also known as a sub-query.

While joins and other table operations provide computationally superior (i.e. faster) alternatives in many cases, the use of sub-queries introduces a hierarchy in execution which can be useful or sometimes necessary.

In the following example, the function AVG receives as input the result of a sub-query:

```
SELECT        isbn,
              title,
              price
FROM          books
WHERE         price < (SELECT AVG(price)
                       FROM books)
ORDER BY      title;
```

3.6.4 Correlated sub-queries: Correlated sub-queries can be a little difficult to comprehend at first, but they crop up quite often so it's worth spending some time learning how these are constructed.

A sub-query can use values from the outer query. In this case, it is known as a correlated sub-query.

You can reference the outer query inside the correlated sub-query using an alias, which makes it quite handy to use (and understand).

In this example, we select all employees whose salary is less than the average of all the employees' salaries in the same department.

```
SELECT        ename,
              sal,
              deptno
FROM          emp a
WHERE         a.sal < (SELECT AVG(sal)
                       FROM emp b
                       WHERE a.deptno = b.deptno)
ORDER BY      deptno;
```

Notice the use of aliases here: In the outer query, the table EMP has an alias 'a' and in the sub-query it is given an alias 'b'. This is done to distinguish the use of the EMP table in the two separate queries.

26

Obviously the aliases need to be different. The sub-query uses the two aliases to make the join to the correlated parent query. The value of the aliases is irrelevant - they can be given any unique legal name.

3.6.5 Comparisons with NULL: The concept of NULL was introduced into SQL to handle missing information in the relational model. The word NULL is a reserved word in SQL. Comparisons with NULL can be made in WHERE clauses for any specific column in a table.

```
SELECT      *
FROM        customers
WHERE       sales is NULL
```

This query will return all CUSTOMER records where the column SALES is NULL.

3.7 SQL Data Modification Language syntax (DML)

Naturally queries are only one component of the SQL language. In order to be able to query data in a table in an Oracle database, you first must get the data into that table. Data is also sometimes deleted from a table and existing data in a table may also sometimes be altered.

The SQL language provides language syntax to permit all such transactions. The part of SQL which deals with these kinds of "transactional" operations is called Data Modification Language - because it deals only with the modification of data in the database.

As we have mentioned already, the three components of "data modification" are as follows:

INSERT:	New data is added to a database table.
UPDATE:	Existing data is altered in a database table.
DELETE:	Existing data is deleted from a database
MERGE INTO:	A combination of INSERT and UPDATE (Also important but less used is the DML syntax MERGE).

3.7.1 Commit and Rollback:

Important concepts in data modification are those of "commit" and "rollback". In Oracle, transactions are said to use a two-phase commit protocol. This means that when a SQL DML command is issued (like an INSERT statement), the statement is parsed and, (provided all is valid), the data prepared for the transaction. However, the transaction is only completed when a "commit" is issued. Similarly an

27

"uncommitted" transaction can be abandoned using the "rollback" command.

Commit and Rollback are extremely important in transaction processing systems when using the DML commands INSERT, UPDATE and DELETE. For example, during an UPDATE or DELETE, the records affected by the transaction are effectively "locked" until the transaction is completed using a "commit" command or abandoned using a "rollback" command. This means that during this period, other users are unable to UPDATE or DELETE these records. This may create contention between other users to get access to alter these records.

For this reason, it is always recommended to issue a "commit" or "rollback" command as soon as possible after a transaction in a program, using UPDATE, DELETE or MERGE commands. Failure to do so can cause locking contention for other users of the data. The programming rule to avoid such contention is "Lock Late - Commit Early".

Later in this volume we will revisit COMMIT and ROLLBACK and give more guidance about how and when they should be used in transactional software.

3.7.2 INSERT Syntax: The INSERT INTO statement is used to insert new records into a table. It is possible to write the INSERT INTO statement in two forms:

a/ The first form does not specify the column names where the data will be inserted. It specifies only their values:

    INSERT INTO   table_name
    VALUES   (value1,value2,value3,...);

b/ The second form specifies the column names and the values to be inserted:

    INSERT INTO   table_name (column1,column2,column3,...)
    VALUES   (value1,value2,value3,...);

3.7.3 UPDATE Syntax: The UPDATE statement is used to update existing records in a table as in the following example:

```
UPDATE      table_name
SET         column1 = value1,
            column2 = value2,..
WHERE       a_column = some_value;
```

Notice the WHERE clause in the SQL UPDATE statement: The WHERE clause specifies which record or records should be updated. If you omit the WHERE clause, all records will be updated.

Here is a simple example of an UPDATE statement:

```
UPDATE      customers
SET         contact_name = 'Andrew Brown',
            city = 'AMSTERDAM'
WHERE       customer_name = 'ORACLE NETHERLANDS';
```

The WHERE clause of an UPDATE statement can be extremely complex and take advantage of the full SQL query syntax we have already described, including sub-queries, correlated sub-queries, multi-table joins etc.

3.7.4 DELETE Syntax: The DELETE statement is used to delete records in a table as follows:

```
DELETE FROM     table_name
WHERE           a_column=some_value;
```

Notice the WHERE clause in the SQL DELETE statement. The WHERE clause specifies which record or records should be deleted. If you omit the WHERE clause, all records will be deleted.

Here is a simple example of a DELETE statement:

```
DELETE      customers
WHERE       customer_name = 'ORACLE NETHERLANDS';
```

The WHERE clause of an DELETE statement can be extremely complex and takes advantage of the full SQL query syntax we have already described, including sub-queries, correlated sub-queries, multi-table joins etc.

3.7.5 MERGE INTO Syntax: MERGE INTO is used when two datasets are to be merged into what used to be referred to as an "UPSERT".

Using MERGE is exactly like an INSERT when the data in the source dataset is completely new data. In this case, this new data is simply INSERTed to the target table.

However, MERGE becomes very useful when *some* data in the source dataset *already* exists in the target dataset - i.e. the data to be INSERTed already exists in the target table. In this event, a MERGE will update the existing data with the new data set. MERGE isn't that common a requirement in software developments but the MERGE INTO syntax can make an otherwise complex programmatic problem much simpler and often more efficient. Prior to the release of MERGE syntax in Oracle, the problem of UPSERT had to be addressed with some pretty inefficient procedural code and cursor handling. Later we will explain why this procedural approach may be undesirable from a performance point of view. Generally speaking the use of MERGE is better that using a PL/SQL explicit cursor.

Here is the general form of MERGE INTO syntax:

```
MERGE   INTO   TABLE_NAME   USING   table_ref   ON
(condition)
WHEN MATCHED THEN
        UPDATE SET column1 = value1 [, column2 = value2
...]
WHEN NOT MATCHED THEN
        INSERT (column1 [, column2 ...]) VALUES (value1 [, value2
...
```

And here is an example of MERGE in action:

```
MERGE INTO bonus b
USING (
        SELECT employee_id, salary, dept_no
        FROM employee
        WHERE dept_no =22) e
ON (b.employee_id = e.employee_id)
WHEN MATCHED THEN
        UPDATE SET b.bonus = e.salary * 0.11
        DELETE WHERE (e.salary < 39000)
WHEN NOT MATCHED THEN
        INSERT (b.employee_id, b.bonus)
        VALUES (e.employee_id, e.salary * 0.10)
        WHERE (e.salary > 49000);
```

3.8 SQL Data Definition Language Syntax (DDL)

Data Definition Language (DDL) is the SQL syntax vocabulary used to define data structures in relational databases like Oracle. It uses a set of specific SQL statements to create, alter, or drop data structures in an instance of an Oracle database.

Obviously, before any data can be queried or inserted to a database, the database itself must exist and be defined to store data in various tables, with specific definitions.

These data structures, like tables, indexes etc., are defined using the DDL component of SQL. Generally speaking, the use of DDL is confined to the DBA group within a development project or a production environment. Normal users and even software developers have a limited (or zero) access to DDL commands.

In addition to the definition of basic data storage objects like tables, DDL syntax is also used to define a myriad of other database objects which may be used to improve performance, guarantee data integrity, define data storage, store PL/SQL (or other executable code) and define all the many other functions of a working database.

The most basic commands of DDL are the CREATE, ALTER, RENAME, DROP and TRUNCATE statements:

CREATE	Creates a new database object.
ALTER	Alters an existing database object.
RENAME	Renames an existing database object.
DROP	Drops an existing database object.
TRUNCATE	Removes all the data from a table instantly (almost).

Note that DDL commands do NOT need to be followed by a COMMIT and they cannot be reversed using ROLLBACK.

We will now take a more detailed look at the basic DDL:

3.8.1 CREATE - Creates a new database object: The CREATE command may be used to create many different database objects. Here is a short list of database objects which may be created using this command:

CREATE DATABASE...

CREATE TABLE....

CREATE INDEX....

CREATE VIEW....

CREATE TRIGGER....

CREATE PROCEDURE...

Here are some examples of the syntax used:

3.8.1.1 Example of the DDL CREATE statement:

CREATE TABLE: Here is an example of the statement to CREATE a table. The Basic syntax of CREATE TABLE statement is as follows:

CREATE TABLE	table_name
(COLUMN1	datatype,
COLUMN2	datatype,
COLUMN3	datatype,
COLUMNn	datatype);

CREATE TABLE tells the database that you want to create a new table. The unique name or identifier for the table follows the CREATE TABLE statement. Then in brackets comes the list defining each column in the table and its data type:

CREATE TABLE	customers(
customer_id	VARCHAR2(10) NOT NULL,
cust_name	VARCHAR2(20) NOT NULL,
address	VARCHAR(60));

You can verify if your table has been created successfully by looking at the message displayed by the SQL server or you can use DESC command at the SQL> prompt:

SQL> desc customers

An alternative and useful form of the CREATE statement is the CREATE OR REPLACE statement. Normally, a CREATE statement will fail if the object already exists. However, with this variant, if the object does not exist, it will be created and if it does exist, it will be replaced *without* any error occurring.

3.8.2 ALTER - Alters an existing database object: The ALTER command may be used against all database objects. The syntax varies according to the type of ALTER being executed but the typical syntax is as follows:

ALTER objecttype objectname parameters.

3.8.2.1 Example of the DDL ALTER statement:

    ALTER TABLE   employees
    DROP COLUMN   date_of_birth;

Here the table EMPLOYEES is to be altered and the column DATE_OF_BIRTH is to be dropped. Columns can also be added, and altered (with some obvious restrictions).

3.8.3 RENAME - Renames an existing database object: Use the RENAME statement to rename a table, view, sequence, or private synonym. For example:

    RENAME departments TO old_departments;

This example renames the table DEPARTMENTS to OLD_DEPARTMENTS.

The Oracle Database automatically transfers integrity constraints, indexes, and grants on the old object to the new object, but it invalidates all objects that depend on the renamed object, such as views, synonyms, and stored procedures and functions that refer to a renamed table. In this case these associated objects need to be COMPILED again to make them valid again, using a script with a form as follows:

    ALTER PACKAGE   my_package   COMPILE;
    ALTER PACKAGE   my_package   COMPILE
    ALTER PROCEDURE   my_procedure   COMPILE;
    ALTER FUNCTION   my_function   COMPILE;
    ALTER TRIGGER   my_trigger   COMPILE;
    ALTER VIEW   my_view   COMPILE;

Note: You cannot use this statement directly to rename columns. However, you can rename a column using the

    ALTER TABLE ... rename_column_clause.

3.8.4 DROP - Drops an existing database object: The drop command is used to completely remove a database object. If this happens to be a table, this will also remove the table data of course.

A DROP statement in SQL removes an object from the data dictionary of the database. Typical usage of the drop command is as follows:

    DROP objecttype objectname

For example, the command to drop a table named EMPLOYEES would be:

DROP TABLE cmployees;

The DROP statement should not be confused with the DELETE and TRUNCATE statements. The DELETE and TRUNCATE commands do not remove the table itself. For example, a DELETE statement might delete some (or all) data from a table while leaving the table itself defined in the database, whereas a DROP statement would remove the entire table from the database.

3.8.5 TRUNCATE - Removes all the data from a table almost instantly: TRUNCATE is used to remove all data from a table. TRUNCATE always removes all rows from a table. The operation cannot be rolled back and no triggers will be fired, which makes TRUNCATE faster than a normal DELETE. TRUNCATE also doesn't use as much "undo" space as a DELETE. Here is an example of the TRUNCATE syntax:

TRUNCATE TABLE emp;

3.9 SQL Data Command Language syntax (DCL)

The Data Control Language (DCL) authorizes users to access and manipulate data. Its two main statements are:

- GRANT authorizes one or more users to perform an operation or a set of operations on an object.

- REVOKE eliminates a grant, which may be the default grant.

Examples:

```
GRANT      SELECT, UPDATE
ON         my_table
TO         a_user, b_user;
and
REVOKE     SELECT, UPDATE
ON         my_table
FROM       a_user, b_user;
```

3.10 SQL Data Types in Oracle

Oracle has a particular range of datatypes, some of which you can also find in other relational databases, but some of which are peculiar to Oracle. Here are some common datatypes and a short definition of their use:

Character Datatypes: These datatypes are used to store character data:

CHAR	Up to 2000 bytes, fixed length, blank
VARCHAR2	Up to 4000 bytes, variable length, saves
LOB Character	Up to 8 terabytes of character data

Number Datatypes: The datatype used to store character data is NUMBER. The NUMBER datatype stores fixed and floating-point numbers. Numbers of virtually any magnitude can be stored and are guaranteed portable among different systems within the Oracle Database, up to 38 digits of precision.

Here are some typical formats:

NUMBER	Stores complete number
NUMBER(9)	Stores number to max length 9
NUMBER(9,2)	Stores number max length 9 and 2 dec. places

Date Datatype: Oracle is especially good at handling dates and times. The DATE datatype is used to store point-in-time values (dates and times) in a table.

The DATE datatype stores the year (including the century), the month, the day, the hours, the minutes, and the seconds (starting at midnight of the date). Oracle DATE columns always contain fields for both date and time. If your queries use a date format without a time portion, then you must ensure that the time fields in the DATE column are set to midnight.

An Oracle Database can store dates in the Julian era, ranging from January 1, 4712 BCE through December 31, 9999 CE (Common Era, or 'AD'). Unless BCE ('BC' in the format mask) is specifically used, CE date entries are the default.

Oracle uses its own internal format to store dates. Date data is stored in fixed-length fields of seven bytes each, corresponding to century, year, month, day, hour, minute, and second.

For input and output of dates, the standard Oracle date format is DD-MON-YY, as follows: '13-NOV-92'

---o0o---

4. Complex SQL constructs: Understanding Joins

4.1 SQL Joins: A SQL join is used to combine rows from multiple tables. A SQL join is performed whenever two or more tables are listed in the SQL FROM clause of a SQL statement. There are several different kinds of SQL join:

- SQL Simple Inner joins
- SQL Outer joins
- SQL Cartesian joins
- SQL Non equi-joins

Let's look at the differences between these joins.

4.1.1 SQL Inner joins (aka an Equi-join): The most common type of SQL join is the simple inner join. SQL inner joins return all rows from multiple tables where the join condition is "true".

Normally, tables are joined when they are related to each other, for example in the way that ORDERS are related to SUPPLIERS. These tables would be joined using the Foreign Key column(s) of the ORDERS table to the Primary Key column(s) of the SUPPLIERS table.

For example, here we will extract SUPPLIERS and ORDERS data by joining these 2 related tables on the referential keys (Foreign key: ORDERS.SUPPLIER_ID joined to Primary key: SUPPLIERS.SUPPLIER_ID):

```
SELECT      suppliers.supplier_id,
            suppliers.supplier_name,
            orders.order_date
FROM        suppliers,
            orders
WHERE       suppliers.supplier_id = orders.supplier_id;
```

This inner join example would return all rows from the SUPPLIERS and ORDERS tables but only where there is a matching SUPPLIER_ID value in both the SUPPLIERS and ORDERS tables.

Let's look at some data to explain how SQL inner joins work:

We have a table called SUPPLIERS with two fields (SUPPLIER_ID and SUPPLIER_ NAME). It contains the following data:

supplier_id	supplier_name
1000	Ford
1001	Mercedes
1002	Toyota
1003	Nissan

We have another table called ORDERS with three fields (ORDER_ID, SUPPLIER_ID, and ORDER_DATE). It contains the following data:

order_id	supplier_id	order_date
50125	1000	12/07/2012
50126	1001	13/05/2009

If we run the SQL statement (that contains an inner join) below:

```
SELECT      suppliers.supplier_id,
            suppliers.supplier_name,
            orders.order_date
FROM        suppliers,
            orders
WHERE       suppliers.supplier_id = orders.supplier_id;
```

Our result set would look like this:

supplier_id	name	order_date
1000	Ford	12/07/2012
1001	Mercedes	13/05/2009

The rows for "Toyota" and "Nissan" from the SUPPLIERS table would be omitted since the SUPPLIER_ID's 1002 and 1003 do not exist in both tables. This is what makes an Inner Join different from an Outer Join, as we shall see.

4.1.2 SQL Outer joins: Another type of join is called an SQL Outer join. This type of join will also return *non-matched* rows from joined tables.

Traditionally in Oracle SQL, the table which is deficient in matching records is marked with a "+" in Oracle SQL. Oracle 9i introduced the ANSI syntax of LEFT OUTER JOIN and RIGHT OUTER JOIN as an alternative syntax.

Here are some examples using the (slightly simpler) legacy syntax (+):

```
SELECT      e.ename,
            d.dname
FROM        emp e,
            dept d
WHERE       e.deptno = d.deptno(+);
```

or

```
SELECT      e.ename,
            d.dname
FROM        emp e,
            dept d
WHERE       e.deptno(+) = d.deptno;
```

Here the (+) sign indicates that in case a column contains a null, the row should also be included (matching keys are missing).

To refer again to our earlier (inner join) example, this time we add the outer join (+) symbol where data matches are missing on the ORDERS table part of the join:

```
SELECT      suppliers.supplier_id,
            suppliers.supplier_name,
            orders.order_date
FROM        suppliers,
            orders
WHERE       suppliers.supplier_id = orders.supplier_id(+);
```

This SQL outer join example would return all rows from the suppliers table and only those rows from the orders table where the joined fields are equal.

The (+) after the ORDERS.SUPPLIER_ID field indicates that if a SUPPLIER_ID value in the SUPPLIERS table does not exist in the ORDERS table, all fields in the orders table will display as NULL in the result set.

So let us use the same data we used in the inner join example to explain how SQL outer joins work with the join between SUPPLIERS and ORDERS.

If we run the SQL statement that contains the outer join above, our result set would look like this:

supplier_id	supplier_name	order_date
1000	Ford	12/07/2012

1001	Mercedes	13/05/2009
1002	Toyota	\<NULL\>
1003	Nissan	\<NULL\>

From the result set we can see that all SUPPLIER records are returned, together with all the matching ORDERS data, but also all other SUPPLIER data is returned even when there is no matching ORDERS data. In this case, the ORDER_DATE is represented as \<NULL\> in an outer join.

Note: Remember to place the (+) sign on the side of the join that is *deficient* in matching records, in this case the ORDERS table.

4.1.3 Cartesian Product: A Cartesian product is the result of an unqualified join of every row of one table to every row of another table. This happens when no matching join columns are specified in a WHERE clause.

For example, if table A with 100 rows is referenced in a select statement with table B with 1000 rows, without the tables being joined on a common column, then a Cartesian product will return 100,000 rows. Note: A query must have at least (N-1) join conditions to prevent a Cartesian product, where N is the number of tables in the query. So if there are 3 tables in a join there should be at least 2 join conditions to stop a Cartesian product occurring.

This is really something to be avoided! There are almost no functional reasons to construct a Cartesian join. Mostly, Cartesian products result from sloppy SQL coding or a poor understanding of the relationships between tables.

Poorly constructed code resulting in a Cartesian product can have catastrophic effects on database performance. It is very easy to construct a scenario where two tables of say 10,000 records each, joined in this way could give rise to 100 million record results with a correspondingly huge processing demand on the database server.

Here are 2 simple examples:

```
SELECT      *
FROM        emp,
            dept;
```

and

```
SELECT      *
FROM        emp,
            dept
WHERE       dept.deptno = 10
AND         emp.sal > 10000;
```

Notice that there are no join conditions specified for the 2 tables involved in these queries.

4.1.4 SQL Non Equi-joins: An non Equi (or theta) join is a join statement that uses an unequal operation (i.e: $\Leftrightarrow$, >, <,!=, BETWEEN, etc.) to match rows from different tables. The converse of a non Equi-join is an Equi-join (inner join) operation.

Here is an example:

```
SELECT      e.ename,
            e.sal,
            s.grade
FROM        emp e,
            salgrade s
WHERE       e.sal BETWEEN s.losal and s.hisal;
```

4.2 SQL Hierarchical queries: This is one of the more complex SQL constructs you will encounter. It occurs when a table has a recursive relationship, i.e. data within a table is related to other data within the table in a hierarchical way.

Relational databases do not store data in a hierarchical way and yet sometimes data is related in a hierarchical way: for example, in some cases employees may also be supervisors and managers of other employees, yet all are stored within the same employees table EMP.

Another similar example would be physical components within a sub assembly, where the sub assembly itself is also a component in its own right. Here there are obvious hierarchical relationships involved.

How then can we define and query this kind of data in a hierarchical manner? Fortunately, Oracle provides a hierarchical querying feature - sometimes called "tree walking" - where data can be queried using its natural hierarchic relationships. Tree walking enables us to construct a hierarchical tree if the relationships lie in the same table.

For instance, a manager column which exists in the EMP table defines the managerial hierarchy between employees who are also managers. A simple query will only reveal who is a manager or which employees are managed by a particular manager. Of course, a manager is also an employee and may also have his own manager.

```
SELECT    ename,
          empno,
          mgr
FROM      emp
WHERE     mgr = 7839;
```

ENAME	EMPNO	MGR
JONES	7566	7839
BLAKE	7698	7839
CLARK	7782	7839

But to build a complete hierarchical query we need to use special syntax which is designed to cope with the problem of multiple layers in the hierarchy. The generic syntax to do this is as follows:

```
SELECT...
[START WITH initial_condition]
CONNECT BY [nocycle] PRIOR recurse_condition
[ORDER SIBLINGS BY order_by_clause]
```

Using this special syntax, we can construct a complete hierarchical representation of the data.

In the following example, the hierarchy has been emphasised using some formatting of the output set - but of course this is unnecessary and just helps readability:

```
SELECT        lpad(' ',level*2,' ')||ename   ename,
FROM          emp
START WITH    mgr IS NULL
CONNECT  BY   empno = mgr
PRIOR
```

ENAME	EMPNO	MGR
KING	7839	
JONES	7566	7839
SCOTT	7788	7566
ADAMS	7876	7788
FORD	7902	7566
SMITH	7369	7902
BLAKE	7698	7839
ALLEN	7499	7698
WARD	7521	7698
MARTIN	7654	7698
TURNER	7844	7698
JAMES	7900	7698
CLARK	7782	7839
MILLER	7934	7782

Here we explain the use of these keywords:

- START WITH: The row(s) to be used as the root of the hierarchy.

- CONNECT BY: Condition that identifies the relationship between parent and child rows of the hierarchy.

- NOCYCLE: Do not circle around loops (where the current row has a child which is also its ancestor).

- ORDER SIBLINGS BY: Preserve ordering of the hierarchical query then apply the "ORDER_BY"_clause to the sibling rows.

Operators:

- PRIOR - Most commonly used when comparing column values with the equality operator. PRIOR identifies the parent row in the column. The PRIOR keyword can be on either side of the = operator. CONNECT BY PRIOR id=parentid will return different results to CONNECT BY PRIOR parentid=id

- Operators other than the equal sign (=) are theoretically possible in CONNECT BY clauses. However, this can result in an infinite loop through the possible combinations.

- CONNECT_BY_ROOT - When you qualify a column with this operator, Oracle returns the column value using data from the root row. This operator extends the functionality of the CONNECT BY [PRIOR] condition of hierarchical queries. (Oracle 10g)

Pseudo-columns

- LEVEL - Returns a number indicating the level in the hierarchy: 1 for a root row, 2 for a child of a root, and so on.

New pseudo-columns available in Oracle 10g include:

- CONNECT_BY_ISCYCLE - This pseudo column returns 1 if the current row has a child which is also its ancestor (otherwise 0.)

- CONNECT_BY_ISLEAF - Returns 1 if the current row is a leaf of the tree defined by the CONNECT BY condition (otherwise 0.). This pseudo column indicates that a row can be further expanded.

---o0o---

5. Understanding Commit and Rollback

The first important thing to understand about Commit and Rollback is that they only apply to DML statements. They have no meaning in Queries, DDL or DCL statements.

5.1 The concept of Commit in Transaction processing: The COMMIT statement makes permanent any changes made to the database during the current transaction. A commit also makes the changes visible to other users.

When an UPDATE or DELETE statement is issued in SQL (or PL/SQL), the records involved in the transaction are locked until the transaction is committed (or rolled back). This means that no other user can execute an UPDATE or DELETE against these records during the period of the transaction before it is committed.

To the session user that issues an INSERT, UPDATE or DELETE, the transaction will appear to be completed even *before* it is committed. However, to all other users, the data will look the way it did before the INSERT, UPDATE or DELETE until the transaction is committed by the user session that initiated the transaction.

The COMMIT statement releases all row and table locks for the current session, and erases any savepoints marked since the last commit or rollback. Until your changes are committed:

- You can see the changes when you query the tables you modified, but other users cannot see the changes.

- If you change your mind or need to correct a mistake, you can use the ROLLBACK statement to roll back (undo) the changes.

5.2 Rollback in Transaction processing: After having issued an INSERT, UPDATE, DELETE statement, it may be that the transaction should not proceed for some reason.

If this is the case, then the initiating session can issue a ROLLBACK statement. This undoes the transaction and releases all record-level locks on the data as if the transaction never occurred.

Of course, a transaction which has already been committed CANNOT be rolled back!

---o0o---

6. Basic architecture: PL/SQL Procedures, Functions and Triggers

6.1 Introduction to PL/SQL (Procedural Language/Structured Query Language): PL/SQL is Oracle Corporation's procedural extension language for SQL and the Oracle database. Oracle Corporation customarily extends package functionality with each successive release of PL/SQL for the Oracle Database.

PL/SQL's general syntax resembles that of Ada or Pascal. It is also one of three key programming languages embedded in the Oracle Database, along with SQL itself and Java.

PL/SQL supports variables, conditions, loops and exceptions. Arrays are also supported, though in a somewhat unusual way, involving the use of PL/SQL collections. Implementations from version 8 of Oracle Database onwards have included features associated with object-orientation.

Once PL/SQL program units have been stored into the database, they become available for execution at a later time by any privileged user-process.

PL/SQL normally embodies QUERY and DML transaction processing statements, but it can also include DDL statements. PL/SQL also supports dynamic SQL where whole SQL statements can be synthesized programmatically, according to defined functional conditions, and then executed by the calling program.

6.2 The advantages of using PL/SQL:

- **Block Structures:** PL/SQL consists of blocks of code, which can be nested within each other. Each block forms a unit of a task or a logical module. PL/SQL Blocks can be stored in the database and reused.

- **Procedural Language Capability:** PL/SQL consists of procedural language constructs such as conditional statements (if-then-else statements) and loops like (FOR loops). There are other procedural languages available to execute SQL statements against an Oracle database but PL/SQL is preferred in general.

- **Better Performance:** The PL/SQL engine processes multiple SQL statements simultaneously as a single block, thereby reducing network traffic.

- **Error Handling:** PL/SQL handles errors or exceptions effectively during the execution of a PL/SQL program. Once an exception is caught, specific actions can be taken, depending upon the type of exception or it can be displayed to the user with a message.

6.3 A Simple PL/SQL Block:

Each PL/SQL program consists of SQL and PL/SQL statements which form a PL/SQL block. A PL/SQL Block consists of three sections:

- The Declaration section (optional).
- The Execution section (mandatory).
- The Exception (or Error) Handling section (optional).

Declaration Section:

The Declaration section of a PL/SQL Block starts with the reserved keyword DECLARE. This section is optional and is used to declare any placeholders like variables, constants, records and cursors which are used to manipulate data in the execution section. Placeholders may be any of Variables, Constants and Records which stores data temporarily. Cursors are also defined in this section.

Execution Section:

The Execution section of a PL/SQL Block starts with the reserved keyword BEGIN and ends with END. This is a mandatory section and is the section where the program logic is written to perform any task. The programmatic constructs like loops, conditional statements and SQL statements comprise the execution section.

Exception Section:

The Exception section of a PL/SQL Block starts with the reserved keyword EXCEPTION. This section is optional. Any errors in the program can be handled in this section so that the PL/SQL Blocks terminates gracefully. If the PL/SQL Block contains exceptions that cannot be handled, the Block terminates abruptly with errors.

Every statement in the above three sections must end with a semicolon ";".

PL/SQL blocks can be nested within other PL/SQL blocks. Comments can be used to document code. This is how a sample PL/SQL block looks:

```
DECLARE
```

Variable declaration
BEGIN
            Program Execution
EXCEPTION
            Exception handling
END;

6.4 Implementing PL/SQL: Normally PL/SQL is stored and executed from within an Oracle database. It may be defined and stored as one of the following objects:

- **Stored Procedure:** Small PL/SQL programs stored in the database and called for a specific task. May return one or more values or may not.

- **Function:** Similar to a procedure, but can be used with a SQL statement like a built-in SQL function and always returns a value.

- **Database Trigger:** PL/SQL programs stored in the database and executed only as a result of a database event like a record UPDATE or other database event.

- **Database Package:** Packages are groups of conceptually linked functions, procedures, variables, PL/SQL table and record TYPE statements, constants, cursors etc. Packages are often useful for modularising code and improving execution performance.

6.4.1 Stored Procedures: What is a Stored Procedure? A Stored Procedure is a named PL/SQL block which performs one or more specific tasks. This is similar to a procedure in other programming languages.

A procedure has a header and a body. The header consists of the name of the procedure and the parameters or variables passed to the procedure. The body consists of a declaration section, execution section and exception section, similar to a general PL/SQL Block. A procedure is similar to an anonymous PL/SQL Block but it is named for repeated usage.

We can pass parameters to procedures in three ways:

            IN-parameters

            OUT-parameters

            IN OUT-parameters

A procedure may or may not return any value to the process that calls it.

The general Syntax to create a procedure is:

CREATE [OR REPLACE] PROCEDURE proc_name [list of parameters] IS
    Declaration section
BEGIN
    Execution section
EXCEPTION
    Exception section
END;

The syntax within the brackets [ ] indicate they are optional. By using CREATE OR REPLACE together, the procedure is created if no other procedure with the same name exists or the existing procedure is replaced with the current code.

IS - marks the beginning of the body of the procedure and is similar to DECLARE in anonymous PL/SQL Blocks. The code between IS and BEGIN forms the Declaration section.

The example below creates a procedure called 'employer_details' which gives the details of the employee.

```
CREATE          OR          REPLACE          PROCEDURE
        employer_details
IS
CURSOR          emp_cur IS
        SELECT first_name,
        last_name,
        salary
        FROM emp_tbl;
emp_rec          emp_cur%rowtype;
BEGIN
        FOR emp_rec in sales_cur
                LOOP
                dbms_output.put_line(emp_cur.first_name || ' '
||emp_cur.last_name   || ' ' ||emp_cur.salary);
                END LOOP;
END;
/
```

How to execute a Stored Procedure?

There are two ways to execute a procedure.

- From the SQL prompt: EXECUTE [or EXEC] procedure_name.

- From within another procedure - simply use the procedure name.

NOTE: In the examples given above, we are using backward slash '/' at the end of the program. This indicates to the oracle engine that the PL/SQL program has ended and it can begin processing the statements.

6.4.2 Functions: What is a Function in PL/SQL? A function is a named PL/SQL Block which is similar to a procedure. The major difference between a procedure and a function is that a function must always return a value when it is called whereas a procedure may or may not return a value. The general syntax to create a function is as follows:

```
CREATE  [OR  REPLACE]  FUNCTION  function_name
[parameters]
        RETURN return_datatype;
IS
        Declaration_section
BEGIN
        Execution_section
        Return return_variable;
EXCEPTION
        exception section
        Return return_variable;
END;
```

Return Type: The header section defines the return type of the function. The return datatype can be any of the Oracle datatype like varchar, number etc. The execution and exception section should both return a value which is of the datatype defined in the header section.

For example, let's create a function called 'employer_details_func' similar to the one created in the stored procedure above:

```
CREATE OR REPLACE FUNCTION employer_details_func
        RETURN VARCHAR(20);
IS emp_name VARCHAR(20);
BEGIN
        SELECT first_name
        INTO emp_name
        FROM emp_tbl
        WHERE empid = '100';
RETURN emp_name;
EXCEPTION
```

```
            WHEN    OTHERS    THEN    RETURN    'ERROR
RAISED';
END;
/
```

In the example we are retrieving the 'first_name' of employee with empid = 100 to variable 'emp_name'. The return type of the function is VARCHAR which is declared in line 2. The function returns the 'emp_name' which is of type VARCHAR, as in the return value. Any type of exception will cause the RETURN value to be set to "ERROR RAISED".

How to execute a PL/SQL Function? A function can be executed in the following ways:

- Since a function returns a value we can assign it to a variable.

   employee_name := employer_details_func;

   If 'employee_name' is of datatype VARCHAR we can store the name of the employee by assigning the return type of the function to it.

- As a part of a SELECT statement

   SELECT employer_details_func
   FROM dual;

- In a PL/SQL Statements like:

   dbms_output.put_line(employer_details_func);

   This will display the value returned by the function.

6.4.3 Database Triggers: What is a Trigger? A DML trigger is a PL/SQL block structure which is fired when a DML statement like INSERT, DELETE, UPDATE is executed on a database table. Therefore a trigger can be defined to execute automatically when an associated DML statement is executed successfully.

Triggers are often used to cascade transactional data to "summary" tables. For example, an invoicing system might recalculate INVOICE LINE totals to update an INVOICE HEADER table or an ACCOUNTS PAYABLE table whenever an INVOICE LINE is inserted, updated or deleted.

The general syntax for the creation of a DML trigger is as follows:

   CREATE [OR REPLACE] TRIGGER trigger_name

```
{BEFORE | AFTER | INSTEAD OF }
{INSERT [OR] | UPDATE [OR] | DELETE}
OF col_name]
ON table_name
[REFERENCING OLD AS o NEW AS n]
[FOR EACH ROW]
WHEN (condition)
BEGIN
  --- sql statements
END;
```

The syntax for a DML Database Trigger is quite flexible and therefore complicated, but here are some explanations for some of the more often used syntax:

- **CREATE [OR REPLACE] TRIGGER trigger_name** - This clause creates or overwrites an existing trigger.

- **{BEFORE | AFTER | INSTEAD OF}** - This clause indicates at what point in a database event the trigger should be fired, for example, before or after updating a table. Specify INSTEAD OF to cause the database to fire the trigger instead of executing the triggering event itself.

- **{INSERT [OR] | UPDATE [OR] | DELETE}** - This clause determines the database triggering event. More than one triggering events can be specified together in the same trigger, separated by the OR keyword. The trigger gets fired at all the specified triggering events.

- **[OF col_name]** - This is used with UPDATE triggers when you want to trigger an event only when a specific column is updated.

- **[ON table_name]** - This clause identifies the name of the table or view with which the trigger is associated.

- **[REFERENCING OLD AS 'o' NEW AS 'n']** - This clause is used to reference the old and new values of data being changed in an UPDATE. By default, you reference the values as: old.column_name or: new.column_name. The reference names can also be changed from old (or new) to any other user-defined name.

- You cannot reference old values when inserting a record, or new values when deleting a record, because they do not exist (obviously).

- **[FOR EACH ROW]** - This clause is used to determine whether a trigger must fire when each row gets affected (i.e. a Row-Level Trigger) or just once when the entire SQL statement is executed (i.e. a Statement-Level Trigger).

- **WHEN (condition)** - This is valid only for row level triggers. The trigger is fired only for rows that satisfy the condition specified in the WHEN clause.

Note 1: When an underlying event like an INSERT, UPDATE, DELETE fails for some reason or is ROLLED BACK, then all the transactions of dependent triggers are also rolled back. It's all or nothing and this maintains data integrity very neatly.

Note 2: There is an order of Trigger execution, which is as follows:

1st	All BEFORE statement triggers
2nd	All BEFORE row triggers
3rd	All AFTER row triggers
4th	All AFTER statement triggers

Note 3: DDL triggers are also possible, which "fire" as a result of various DDL statements. These tend to be in the domain of Database and Server administration rather than software development.

Note 4: Cyclic Cascading in a Trigger: This is an undesirable situation where more than one trigger enters into an infinite loop. When designing a trigger we should ensure that such looping cannot occur. This situation will result in an irresolvable error. The following example shows how a trigger can cause cyclic cascading:

Let's consider we have two tables 'ABC' and 'XYZ'. Two triggers are created.

> - The INSERT trigger, TRIGGER_A on table 'ABC' issues an UPDATE on table 'XYZ'.

> - The UPDATE trigger, TRIGGER_B on table 'XYZ' issues an INSERT on table 'ABC'.

In such a situation, when there is a row inserted in table 'ABC', TRIGGER_A fires and will update table 'XYZ'. Then, when the table 'XYZ' is updated, TRIGGER_B fires and will insert a row in table 'ABC' and so on. This will rapidly result in a resource error at the database user level.

6.4.4 An example of a Database Trigger: Here is a simple database trigger. In this example, a food product cost is updated whenever a new raw material is INSERTED or an existing raw material is UPDATED. This is typical of the use of database triggers in maintaining the synchronicity of associated data which is not directly related referentially. In a similar way, Database Triggers are also used to maintain database audit trails which may be maintained in separate secure schema:

```
CREATE OR REPLACE TRIGGER product_ingredients_t3
BEFORE INSERT OR UPDATE OF
        raw_material_ref,
        quantity, raw_material_percent_of_total,
        unit_of_measure
ON product_ingredients
FOR EACH ROW
-- PL/SQL Block
BEGIN
  DECLARE
    v_cost_price_uom NUMBER;
    v_material_cost_per_unit NUMBER;
  BEGIN
    SELECT nvl(cost_price_uom,0)
    INTO v_cost_price_uom
    FROM raw_materials
    WHERE material_code = :new.raw_material_ref;
  v_material_cost_per_unit                                    :=
v_cost_price_uom*((:new.raw_material_percent_of_total/100)
*:new.quantity);
    :new.material_cost_per_unit := v_material_cost_per_unit;
EXCEPTION
  WHEN NO_DATA_FOUND THEN NULL;
END;
END;
```

---o0o---

7. Basic PL/SQL Language syntax

7.1 Main Features of PL/SQL: PL/SQL combines the dataset manipulating power of SQL with the processing power of traditional procedural languages.

Like other procedural programming languages, PL/SQL lets you declare constants and variables, control program flow, define subprograms, and trap run-time errors. A developer can break complex problems into easily understandable subprograms, which can be reused in multiple applications simply by calling them. PL/SQL supports the concept of the Object-Relational database by allowing for the storage and execution of the PL/SQL software in the database itself.

Here are the main language components of PL/SQL:

- PL/SQL Blocks
- PL/SQL Input and Output
- PL/SQL Error Handling
- PL/SQL Data Abstraction
- PL/SQL Variables and Constants
- PL/SQL Control Structures
- PL/SQL Subprograms
- PL/SQL Packages (APIs Written in PL/SQL)

Let us take a look at each of these components.

7.2 PL/SQL Blocks

The basic unit of a PL/SQL source program is the block, which groups related declarations and statements.

A PL/SQL block is defined by the keywords DECLARE, BEGIN, EXCEPTION, and END. These keywords partition the block into a declarative part, an executable part, and an exception-handling part. Only the executable part is required.

Declarations are local to the block and cease to exist when the block completes execution, helping to avoid cluttered namespaces for variables and subprograms.

Blocks can be nested. Because a block is an executable statement, it can appear in another block wherever an executable statement is allowed.

Example PL/SQL Block Structure:

> DECLARE - Declarative part (optional)
> -- Declarations of local types, variables, subprograms
> BEGIN - Executable part (required)
>   -- Statements (which can use items declared in declarative part)
> [EXCEPTION -Exception-handling part (optional)
>   -- Exception handlers for exceptions raised in executable part]
> END;

A PL/SQL block can be submitted to an interactive tool (such as SQL*Plus or Enterprise Manager) or embedded in an Oracle Pre-compiler or OCI program. The interactive tool or program executes the block only once. In this case the block is not stored in the database. A named PL/SQL block - a subprogram - can be invoked repeatedly.

7.3 PL/SQL Input and Output

Most PL/SQL input and output (I/O) is through SQL statements that store data in database tables or query those tables. All other PL/SQL I/O is done through APIs, such as the PL/SQL package DBMS_OUTPUT.

To display output passed to DBMS_OUTPUT, you need another program, such as SQL*Plus. To see DBMS_OUTPUT output with SQL*Plus, you must first issue the SQL*Plus command SET SERVEROUTPUT ON.

Other PL/SQL APIs exist for processing I/O to web pages, operating system, files, web servers and mail servers.

Although some of the preceding APIs can accept input as well as display output, they cannot accept data directly from the keyboard. For that we need to use the SQL*Plus commands PROMPT and ACCEPT.

7.4 PL/SQL Error Handling

PL/SQL makes it easy to detect and process error conditions. These are called exceptions. When an error occurs, an exception is raised: normal execution stops and control transfers to special exception-handling code, which comes at the end of any PL/SQL block. Each different exception is processed by a particular exception handler.

PL/SQL exception handling differs from the manual checking that you would do in C programming, where you insert a check to make sure that every operation succeeded. Instead, the checks and calls to error routines are performed automatically, similar to the exception mechanism in Java programming.

Predefined exceptions are raised automatically for certain common error conditions involving variables or database operations. For example, if you try to divide a number by zero, PL/SQL raises the predefined exception ZERO_DIVIDE automatically.

You can define your own exceptions for conditions that you decide are errors, or to correspond to database errors that normally result in ORA-n error messages. When you detect a user-defined error condition, you raise an exception with either a RAISE statement, or the procedure DBMS_STANDARD.RAISE_APPLICATION_ERROR.

Typically, you put an exception handler at the end of a subprogram to handle exceptions that are raised anywhere inside the subprogram. To continue executing from the spot where an exception happens, enclose the code that might raise an exception inside another BEGIN-END block with its own exception handler. For example, you might put separate BEGIN-END blocks around groups of SQL statements that might raise NO_DATA_FOUND, or around arithmetic operations that might raise DIVIDE_BY_ZERO. By putting a BEGIN-END block with an exception handler inside a loop, you can continue executing the loop even if some loop iterations raise exceptions.

7.5 PL/SQL Data Abstraction: Data abstraction lets us work with the essential properties of data without being too involved with the details of the data structures. This means that after we design a data structure, we can focus on designing algorithms that manipulate the data structure, rather than the actual structure details. There are several types of Data abstraction:

Cursors

%TYPE Attribute
%ROWTYPE Attribute
Collections
Records
Object Types

7.5.1 Cursors: A cursor is the term used for a specific private SQL area in which information for processing a specific statement is kept. PL/SQL uses both implicit and explicit cursors. PL/SQL implicitly declares a cursor for all SQL data manipulation statements on a set of rows, including queries that return only one row. For queries that return more than one row, you can explicitly declare a cursor to process the rows individually. An implicit cursor is created with a SQL statement like:

```
SELECT      last_name,
            salary,
            hire_date,
            job_id
FROM        employees
WHERE       employee_id = 110;
```

However, an explicit cursor is defined in PL/SQL

```
CURSOR      c1 IS
SELECT      last_name,
            salary,
            hire_date,
            job_id
FROM        employees
WHERE       employee_id = 110;
```

Explicit cursors are useful because they allow a PL/SQL program to process each row in a cursor of records one by one, based on the values in each record in the cursor. This is not possible in an explicit cursor where all records in the cursor are processed / returned together.

7.5.2 %TYPE Attribute. The %TYPE attribute provides the data type of a variable or database column. This is very useful when declaring variables that are used to hold database values. For instance, in the last example there is a column called LAST_NAME in the table EMPLOYEES.

To declare a variable named v_last_name that has the same data type as column LAST_NAME, we use the dot notation and the %TYPE attribute, as follows in our PL/SQL declaration:

        v_last_name employees.last_name%TYPE;

Declaring v_last_name with %TYPE has two big advantages:

Firstly, you don't need to know the exact data type of the column LAST_NAME. Secondly, if the database definition of the column LAST_NAME gets changed at some future date, perhaps to make it a longer character string, the data type of v_last_name changes accordingly at run time.

This removes a huge dependency between database structure and PL/SQL code and therefore reduces maintenance overheads and future failures and costs.

7.5.3 %ROWTYPE Attribute: In PL/SQL, records are used to group data. A record consists of a number of related fields in which data values can be stored.

The %ROWTYPE attribute provides a record type that represents a row in a table. The record can store an entire row of data selected from the table or fetched from a cursor or cursor variable.

%ROWTYPE is thus similar to %TYPE except that it refers to an entire row of data in columns. So, columns in a database row and the corresponding fields in a record have the same names and data types.

In the following example, you can declare a record named DEPT_REC, whose fields have the same names and data types as the columns in the DEPARTMENTS table:

```
dept_rec departments%ROWTYPE;
```

So, having declared the record, we can use the dot notation to reference fields in the record as follows, here allocating a variable v_deptid to be equal to the DEPARTMENT_ID in the dept_rec record that we just declared.

```
v_deptid := dept_rec.department_id;
```

So, if we then declare a cursor that retrieves the last name, salary, hire date, and job class of an employee, we can use %ROWTYPE to declare a record that stores the same information and refer to the fields in the record in a simple way.

Again, this makes PL/SQL code much more independent of changes in the database structure, such as column length etc.

Here is an example that uses the FETCH statement to assign the value in the LAST_NAME column of the EMPLOYEES table to the last_name field of employee_rec, the value in the salary column is to the salary field, and so on. The PL/SQL program then outputs that employee's name and last name to the terminal:

```
DECLARE
CURSOR c1 IS
SELECT      last_name,
            salary,
            hire_date,
            job_id
FROM employees
WHERE employee_id = 120;
employee_rec c1%ROWTYPE;

BEGIN
OPEN c1;
FETCH c1 INTO employee_rec;
DBMS_OUTPUT.PUT_LINE('Employee      name:      '    ||
employee_rec.last_name);
END;
/

Employee name: Malcolm

SQL>
```

7.5.4 Collections: PL/SQL collection types let us declare high-level data types similar to arrays, sets, and hash tables which are found in other languages.

In PL/SQL, array types are known as varrays (short for variable-size arrays), set types are known as nested tables, and hash table types are known as associative arrays.

Each kind of collection is an ordered group of elements, all of the same type. Each element has a unique subscript that determines its position in the collection. When declaring collections, we use a TYPE definition.

We can also use collections to work with lists of data in a program that are not stored in database tables.

7.5.5 Records: A PL/SQL record is a data structure that can hold data items of different kinds. Records consist of different fields, similar to a row of a database table. PL/SQL can handle the following types of records:

- Table-based records.

60

- Cursor-based records.

- User-defined records.

To access any field of a record, we use the dot (.) operator. This dot operator is coded as a full-stop between the record variable name and the field that we wish to access.

We can pass a record as a subprogram parameter in a very similar way to passing any other variable.

7.5.6 Object Types: PL/SQL allows the definition of an object type, which helps in designing object-oriented database software in Oracle. Objects are created using the CREATE [OR REPLACE] TYPE statement.

7.6 PL/SQL Variables and Constants: A variable is just a name given to a storage area that a program can manipulate. Each variable in PL/SQL has a specific data type, which determines the size and layout of the variable's memory, the range of values that can be stored within that memory and the set of operations that can be applied to the variable.

The name of a PL/SQL variable consists of a letter optionally followed by more letters, numerals, dollar signs, underscores, and number signs and should not exceed 30 characters. By default, variable names are not case-sensitive. You cannot use reserved PL/SQL keywords as a variable name.

PL/SQL allows us to define various type of variables like date/time data types, records, collections etc. which we will describe later. For now, let us look at basic variable types.

PL/SQL variables must be declared in the declaration section or in a package as a global variable. When you declare a variable, PL/SQL allocates memory for the variable's value and the storage location is identified by the variable name.

The general syntax for declaring a variable is:

> variable_name [CONSTANT] datatype [NOT NULL] [:= |
> DEFAULT initial_value]

Where a variable_name is a valid identifier in PL/SQL, datatype must be a valid PL/SQL data type or any user defined data type. A variable can be assigned a constant value here. For example:

> v_book_id   varchar2(25) := '988625562';

7.7 PL/SQL Control Structures: Control structures are the most important PL/SQL extension to SQL. Not only does PL/SQL let us manipulate database data, it also lets us process the data using flow-of-control statements.

The core components of PL/SQL Control are as follows:

- Conditional Control
- Iterative Control
- Sequential Control

7.7.1 Conditional Control: Decision-making structures require that the programmer specify one or more conditions to be evaluated or tested by the program, along with a statement or statements to be executed if the condition is determined to be true, and optionally, other statements to be executed if the condition is determined to be false.

A sequence of statements that uses query results to select alternative actions is common in database applications. Another common sequence of commands inserts or deletes a row only if an associated entry is found in another table.

We can bundle these common command sequences into a PL/SQL block using conditional logic. Here is a simple example conditional sequence taken from a PL/SQL Function:

```
BEGIN
   open c1;
   fetch c1 into monthly_value;
   close c1;
   IF monthly_value <= 4000 THEN
      ILevel := 'Low Income';
   ELSIF monthly_value > 4000 and monthly_value <= 7000
THEN
      ILevel := 'Avg Income';
   ELSIF monthly_value > 7000 and monthly_value <= 15000
THEN
      ILevel := 'Moderate Income';
   ELSE
      ILevel := 'High Income';
   END IF;
   RETURN ILevel;
END;
```

PL/SQL provides the following types of decision-making statements:

IF - THEN statement: The IF statement associates a condition with a sequence of statements enclosed by the keywords THEN and END IF. If the condition is true, the statements get executed and if the condition is false or NULL then the IF statement does nothing.

IF-THEN-ELSE statement: The IF statement adds the keyword ELSE followed by an alternative sequence of statement. If the condition is false or NULL, then only the alternative sequence of statements gets executed. It ensures that either of the sequence of statements is executed.

IF-THEN-ELSIF statement: It allows you to choose between several alternatives.

Case statement: Like the IF statement, the CASE statement selects one sequence of statements to execute. However, to select the sequence, the CASE statement uses a selector rather than multiple Boolean expressions. A selector is an expression whose value is used to select one of several alternatives.

Searched CASE statement: The searched CASE statement has no selector, and its WHEN clauses contain search conditions that yield Boolean values.

Nested IF-THEN-ELSE: You can use one IF-THEN or IF-THEN-ELSIF statement inside (an) other IF-THEN or IF-THEN-ELSIF statement(s).

7.7.2 Iterative Control: There are many situations in which we need to execute a block of code several times. In general, statements are executed sequentially: the first statement in a function is executed first, followed by the second, and so on.

In order to execute the same statement many times, PL/SQL provides the LOOP statement. A loop statement allows us to execute a statement or a group of statements multiple times. Here is a simple example of the syntax in use:

```
FOR cntr IN 1..20
LOOP
   Calcul := cntr * 31;
END LOOP;
```

To create a loop, we place the keyword LOOP before the first statement in the sequence and the keywords END LOOP after the last statement in the sequence. The following example shows the simplest kind of loop, which repeats a sequence of statements continually:

LOOP

-- sequence of statements

END LOOP;

The EXIT-WHEN statement lets us complete a loop if further processing is impossible or undesirable. When the EXIT statement is encountered, the condition in the WHEN clause is evaluated. If the condition is true, the loop completes and control passes to the next statement. Similarly, the CONTINUE-WHEN statement immediately transfers control to the next iteration of the loop when there is no need to continue working on this iteration. GOTO can also be used to transfer control to the labelled statement, though generally it is not advised to use GOTO statements because they make program control difficult to follow.

7.7.3 Sequential Control: The GOTO statement lets us branch to a label in the program unconditionally. The label, an undeclared identifier enclosed by double angle brackets, must precede an executable statement or a PL/SQL block. When executed, the GOTO statement transfers control to the labelled statement or block. GOTO statements are frowned upon because they make program flow control confusing and prone to unpredictable behaviour, but sometimes the GOTO statement is necessary.

7.8 PL/SQL Subprograms: A PL/SQL subprogram is a named PL/SQL block that can be invoked with a set of parameters. PL/SQL has two types of subprograms, procedures and functions. A function returns a result.

We create standalone subprograms at schema level with the SQL statements CREATE PROCEDURE and CREATE FUNCTION. They are compiled and stored in the database, where they can be used by any number of applications connected to the database. When invoked, they are loaded and processed immediately. Subprograms use shared memory, so that only one copy of a subprogram is loaded into memory for execution by multiple users.

Subprograms are useful for improving reusability in PL/SQL because they can obviously be called from any other program as required.

7.9 PL/SQL Packages: These are basically APIs written in PL/SQL. A PL/SQL package bundles logically related types, variables, cursors, and subprograms into a database object called a package. The package defines a simple, clear interface to a set of related subprograms and types that can be accessed by SQL statements.

PL/SQL lets us access many predefined Oracle PL/SQL packages and it allows us to create own packages for specific purposes.

A package usually has two parts: a specification and a body:

- **The specification** defines the application programming interface (API); it declares the types, constants, variables, exceptions, cursors and subprograms. To create a package specification, we use the CREATE PACKAGE Statement.

- **The body** contains the SQL queries for cursors and the code for subprograms. To create a package body, we use the CREATE PACKAGE BODY Statement.

Packages are stored in the database, where they can be shared by many applications. Invoking a packaged subprogram for the first time loads the whole package and caches it in memory, saving on disk I/O for subsequent invocations. Thus, packages enhance reuse and improve performance in a multi-user, multi-application environment.

---o0o---

8. PL/SQL Exception handling.

An error condition during a program execution is called an exception in PL/SQL. PL/SQL supports programmers to catch such conditions using an EXCEPTION block in a PL/SQL program, and an appropriate action is taken against each error condition. There are two types of exceptions:

System-defined exceptions.

User-defined exceptions.

8.1 Syntax for Exception Handling: The general syntax for exception handling is as follows:

```
DECLARE
  <declarations section>
BEGIN
  <executable command(s)>
EXCEPTION
  <exception handling goes here >
  WHEN exception1 THEN
    exception1-handling-statements
  WHEN exception2  THEN
    exception2-handling-statements
  WHEN exception3 THEN
    exception3-handling-statements
  ........
  WHEN others THEN
    exception3-handling-statements
END;
```

Here we can define as many exceptions as we want to handle. The default exception will be handled using WHEN others THEN. This means that all exceptions, which are not explicitly handled, will be handled by the WHEN OTHERS exception clause.

Typical System pre-defined exceptions include the following examples:

- WHEN NO_DATA_FOUND THEN

- WHEN INVALID_NUMBER THEN

- WHEN TOO_MANY_ROWS THEN

- WHEN ZERO_DIVIDE THEN

- WHEN OTHERS THEN

  ………

8.2 Raising Exceptions: Exceptions are raised by the database server automatically whenever there is any internal database error, but exceptions can be raised explicitly by the programmer by using the command RAISE. The following is the simple syntax used to raise an exception:

```
DECLARE
  exception_name EXCEPTION;
BEGIN
  IF condition THEN
    RAISE exception_name;
  END IF;
EXCEPTION
  WHEN exception_name THEN
  statement;
END;
```

You can use the above syntax in raising Oracle standard exceptions or any user-defined exception.

User-defined Exceptions: PL/SQL allows us to define our own exceptions according to the need of a program. A user-defined exception must be declared and then raised explicitly, using either a RAISE statement or the procedure:

DBMS_STANDARD.RAISE_APPLICATION_ERROR.

---o0o---

9. SQL and PL/SQL: some standards for good coding appearance

There are many standards available for coding SQL and PL/SQL, and its worth looking at some of these standards before making a choice about which is best for your project.

Bear in mind that standards can be both a help and a hindrance. If a standard isn't intuitive to the programmers, they won't use it or they will use it wrongly. Standards need to be simple and obvious, both to the future reader of the software and also to the present developer of the software.

On the other hand, it is vital that software is properly and consistently coded across an entire project. Apart from causing future readability problems and maintenance hassles / costs, SQL code which is identical in function but differently coded causes performance degradation when it is executed.

For this reason alone it is really vital to ensure that all reusable components are properly identified for coding as *reusable* units during the software design phase.

What follows is a personalised sample of SQL coding standards. The main topics you need to address in your own SQL coding standards are:

- Readability & Layout
- Naming Standards
- Code Commenting

9.1 Readibility & Layout: Here is a sample set of standards that can be used to improve readability of SQL code.

Note the following when defining your own standards:

- **Whitespace:** Insignificant whitespace is generally ignored in SQL statements and queries, making it easier to format SQL code for readability.

- **Case insensitive:** SQL is not case sensitive: "SELECT" is the same as "select". However the use of case can help readability in large SQL statements.

- **Pick your standard:** There are no universal standards for readability. What we provide here are just suggestions for standards which are in fairly widespread use.

- **Consistency:** Once a set of standards is defined for SQL layout then it should be rigorously adopted. This is because, in some cases, completely identical SQL statements which are coded with a different layout may cause reparsing of the statement, even though the same statement is already in the Oracle SGA. This will hurt performance.

9.1.1 A standard for SQL readability: Here is our suggested standard for SQL and PL/SQL formatting:

- Uppercase all reserved words (such as SELECT, FROM, WHERE), including functions and data types.

- Place one declaration on each line

    DECLARE

    Comp_type VARCHAR2 (3);

    Right_now DATE := SYSDATE;

    Month_num INTEGER;

- Put block delimiters (such as BEGIN and END) on a new line by themselves, correctly indented.

- Keep database objects either all lowercase or all UPPERCASE (tables etc.), but don't mix them. The same goes for column names. Generally it reads better if you keep table and column names lowercase and reserve keywords in uppercase.

- All built-in functions are in uppercase,

    e.g. v_id := TO_CHAR(v_num);

- All built-in package names in uppercase,

    e.g. DBMS_OUTPUT.PUT_LINE(v_out);

- Indent everything within a PL/SQL clause, such as variable declarations, exceptions, loops, conditions etc. Arrange series of statements containing similar operators into columns whenever it will not cause excessive white space and you have sufficient room to do so.

- Use the semicolon to aid the reading of code, even where SQL syntax states that it is only optional.

- Lists and Operators: Always LEFT align clauses, lists of columns, variables, parameters etc. - Put line breaks within SQL statements before the clause (FROM, ON, WHERE, HAVING, GROUP BY). Put a line-break and indent between list items, as in the following examples:

E.g. 1: Parameters, variables, constants, etc. in PL/SQL declarations:

```
v_firstname := 'Lynne';

v_lastname  := 'Brown';
```

E.g. 2: Columns and clauses in SQL statements:

```
SELECT     last_name,
           first_name
FROM       employees
WHERE      department_id = 15
AND        hire_date < sysdate;


INSERT
INTO students (ssn,
               first_name,
               last_name,

               ...
               most_recent_gpa)
VALUES         (999999999,
               'Roger',
               'Smith',

               ...,
               NULL);
```

E.g. 3 Parameter lists and definitions:

```
PROCEDURE    USP_GET_CLNT_LS
             p_idn_case          IN VARCHAR2,
             p_num_days          IN VARCHAR2,
             p_start_date        IN VARCHAR2,
             p_end_date          IN VARCHAR2....
```

9.2 Naming Standards in SQL and PL/SQL:

- Parameters names must begin with p_

- Variable names must begin with v_

- IN parameter can be named _in

- OUT parameter can be named _out

- IN OUT parameters can be named _inout

9.3 Commenting in PL/SQL

9.3.1 Comments in Stored Procedures: A summary is placed at the top of a stored procedure and includes:

- Name of stored procedure, any input/output parameters, calls to other stored procedures.

- A description that contains information on the logic, various modules of the program, and functionality of the stored procedure.

- A summary that also contains a maintenance log that includes: Date of creation / amendment, the person who created / amended the version number, PCR (program change request) number, and an explanation that includes a reason for the initial release or PCR. The PCR number must be referenced with a main explanation of what the PCR is intended to do.

Here is a simple example:

```
/****************************************************
// Program Name: xxx_xxxx_xxxx
//
// Parameter(s) input: Department Number
// Parameter(s) output: Number of employees
//
// Calls: (other stored proc)
//
```

// Description: Returns the number of employees assigned to a given dept. Errors on invalid department. Departments with

// zero employees is NOT an error.

//

// Maintenance log:

// Date Created / Change

//

// 10/12/1999 Jane Doe 1.0.0 Initial release. Provide an overview of what stored procedure //

/**/

9.3.2 Block Comments: Each PL/SQL block can have a simple comment describing its basic functionality. Do this for the future maintenance of the PL/SQL blocks in our software by the next generation of developers that have to live with and understand the software we have designed and coded. It is basic professional courtesy and it can also have a significant future maintenance-cost impact.

As a minimum, describe what the block does functionally, what the incoming and outgoing parameters are and something about the processing algorithm itself.

9.3.3 Incidental Comments: At the discretion of the developer we should include comments to explain any particularly difficult code to future programmers. This "incidental commentary" should be clear and in plain language. Such commentary can be enormously helpful, but we need to remember that more is not necessarily better. So we shouldn't assume that the reader has no understanding of PL/SQL and heap comments in our code. Too much commentary will tend to make the software harder to read. Instead, it is much better to add the occasional, clear comment when the code is becoming a bit esoteric. Try to put yourself in the place of a future maintenance developer that has no idea of the algorithm you have decided to use to build a particular piece of software. Describe the basic approach in the procedure / block and refer to this in incidental comments.

---o0o---

10. Performance considerations when coding in SQL

There are many contributory factors which influence the performance of an Oracle-based system, and we deal with this subject in more detail in a later volume. However, it is generally recognised that one of the most common causes of poor application system performance is badly constructed SQL code. Therefore, we are going to take a brief look at this subject and suggest some ways to avoid the really obvious performance problems. We start with some of the simpler coding, testing and design errors and then take a look at a sample of the more complex performance issues often encountered.

10.1 Performance Test each part of your code: Very often developers are somewhat preoccupied with getting a piece of code to actually work and they tend to overlook performance issues during development. This is a big mistake, because very quickly a group of developers working hard to build thousands of lines of PL/SQL can soon store up an enormous performance problem which only gets discovered when software is being tested prior to release.

Generally, developers work with small sample volumes of data to test functionality and rarely work with production volumes. Thus the performance issue gets deferred and becomes someone else's problem - very often on a grand scale! Project managers tend to contribute to the culture of quantity (of code) rather than quality, because they are operating against tight timescales and issues like quality and performance get squeezed out in the race to tick boxes of "Modules Completed".

Unfortunately, performance problems tend to have a cumulative effect, with several software components contributing to an overall degradation in performance. For example, an inefficient batch processing module may create a poor resource environment for OLTP software execution. The users will blame the OLTP software because that is where they see the performance symptoms, but the reality may well be elsewhere in an unseen inefficient PL/SQL process running in the background "beating up" the database server.

Especially in high volume, multi-user environments, performance problems can and often do rapidly rise to become complete show-stoppers whilst functional issues fade into relative insignificance as mere bugs.

Therefore, it is vital that every module of PL/SQL be individually performance-tested by the developer in just as stringent a way as he or she would be expected to unit test the functionality of a module before passing it as completed. To do this, the project management must provide certain infrastructure to the development team, including the following:

- Several Production Volume test environments (with fast refresh functions for reuse).

- Access to the tools: EXPLAIN PLAN tools (TOAD, SQL Developer etc.) are required to allow the developer to test and optimise the execution plans being used by his code. Oracle has some excellent performance management tools to help guide a developer and DBA to optimise a piece of code.

- A performance specialist to help and advise the development team. Having an outsider specifically to manage system performance and take responsibility for performance *during development* is an essential, not a luxury.

- The sign off for every completed module should include a full performance evaluation including EXPLAIN_PLAN outputs, execution timings, etc. No module should reach production without formalised, documented performance testing.

10.2 Some specific performance considerations when writing SQL

10.2.1 Avoid the dreaded Cartesian join: As we explained above, a Cartesian product occurs when 2 (or more) tables which are referenced in a FROM clause are not joined in the WHERE clause of a SQL statement. There is almost no case where this is a desirable construct in normal software development. In general, if there are two or more tables involved in a select statement, these tables should be unambiguously joined through their appropriate Primary Key and Foreign Key columns. Logically, if there are 2 tables in a select statement, there must be at least 1 join statement.

10.2.2 SQL is not using indexes when they should be used: Indexes exist primarily to improve the performance of queries on large tables. Using an index to select, update or delete a few rows in a big table is orders of magnitude faster than using a table scan.

SQL queries (including UPDATES and DELETES) on large tables should generally use the available indexes to improve performance. However, SQL code can cause indexes to be ignored and give rise to so-called "Full-table scans". This can cause catastrophic performance problems in queries across one or more very large tables. There are several possible reasons for this to happen. Here are a couple of possible scenarios:

- The SQL contains no WHERE clauses referencing an indexed column.

- The SQL refers to an indexed column but is using a negative operator, e.g. using <>, NOT IN, NOT EXISTS etc. Indexes are useful to help us find an existing data record but not useful to tell us what records are *not* in existence.

10.2.3 SQL is using indexes but should not use an index: Often, small tables have indexes which are not designed for performance enhancement. Generally, these indexes are fairly irrelevant to performance, because the table is so small that whether the table is read directly or via the index during a SELECT statement, doesn't impact on performance very much. There is one notable exception to this and that is when a table is being read very, very frequently. In such a case it is preferable to avoid reading the index and simply read the table during the SELECT, UPDATE, DELETE statement. Therefore the programmer needs to ensure that the index is ignored. This can be done using a "hint" (which we will explain later).

10.2.4 SQL query is slow because no index is available: Sometimes it is necessary to request the creation of a completely new index on a table solely in order to improve the performance of a single important, time-critical SQL statement. This is quite legitimate. We need to realise that too many indexes may increase INSERT, UPDATE and DELETE overheads but too few may degrade SELECT performance. Therefore, a balance needs to be established between the bare minimum of indexes (primary, unique and foreign keys) and having too many superficial and rarely used indexes.

10.2.5 Where possible make SQL reusable: The reasons for this are not quite as obvious as it might appear. Because parsing SQL is CPU intensive, we must try to reduce SQL parsing as much as possible. Therefore, code which is common to many modules should be extracted and centralised so that it can be called by other parts of the application. Code which is "almost the same" will always be parsed separately. If it isn't *exactly* the same, it is considered to be "new code" by Oracle and will be unnecessarily parsed. Differences in formatting can cause this to happen.

10.2.6 Minimise SQL parsing in other ways: Do not use literals in SQL statements, instead use bind variables. This will minimize parsing by reusing parsed statements cached in the shared pool.

10.2.7 Process multiple rows at a time whenever possible: Oracle is particularly efficient at set processing of SQL statements. Therefore, where possible, use a single SQL statement to process a group of records together rather than taking a procedural approach of processing one record at a time, if this is not absolutely necessary. In PL/SQL, if we need to use a procedural approach, then design the application to process multiple rows at a time. For example, in PL/SQL we can use the FORALL statement and BULK COLLECT clause together with PL/SQL collection types to implement bulk processing.

10.2.8 Avoid data type conversions: Do not use type conversion functions (such as a TO_DATE or TO_CHAR) on indexed columns. Instead, use the functions against the values being compared to a column. Natural indexes don't store the converted value, so this could cause the index to be ignored by the SQL Optimiser when it comes to execution.

10.2.9 Use correct datatypes: Using incorrect datatypes may decrease the efficiency of the optimiser and degrade performance. It might also cause an application to perform unnecessary data conversions. Don't use a string to store dates, times or numbers. Ensure that conditional expressions compare the same data types.

10.2.10 Avoid Dynamic SQL: It is possible to dynamically create SQL statements according to the needs of a particular process step. The dynamic SQL can then be executed. Whilst this can be hugely convenient sometimes, it may also cause a serious performance issue. This is because SQL statements that are fixed at compile time are usually executed faster and the principle "parse once, execute many times" is automatically applied to them. Also, the PL/SQL compiler automatically 'bulkifies' static SQL to improve performance. Dynamic SQL should be used only when static SQL is no longer practical, e.g. code becomes too complex with static SQL; or when dynamic SQL is the only option.

10.2.11 Optimiser Hints: Sometimes it is necessary to intervene in how the Oracle Optimiser decides to execute a SQL statement. A typical example is when you really do not wish to use a particular index or particularly do want to use a different index. However there are many ways in which a developer can intervene to improve performance of a SQL statement. This is done in practice using "Optimiser hints".

Optimiser hints can be used with SQL statements to alter execution plans. Here is an example of a hint which is telling the optimiser which indexes should be used:

```
SELECT      /*+  index(t1  t1_abc)  index(t2  t2_abc)  */
FROM        t1,
            t2
WHERE       t1.col1 = t2.col1;
```

This is a complex subject with many possible options, but basically "hints" are added to SQL code by the developer to achieve a particular execution plan - normally for reasons of performance improvement. You can use hints to specify the following:

- The optimisation approach for a SQL statement
- The goal of the cost-based optimiser for a SQL statement
- The access path for a table accessed by the statement
- The join order for a join statement
- A join operation in a join statement

Hints provide a mechanism to direct the optimiser to choose a certain query execution plan based on the following criteria:

- Join order
- Join method
- Access path
- Parallelization

---oOo---

11. Installing and using a SQL*Plus client

A typical installation of a SQL*Plus client would be on a MS Windows based PC but the installation is basically the same, regardless of the type of client. There are two basic stages in installing the client:

- PC installation of SQL*Plus client

- Configuration of database connections (TNS configuration)

11.1 Procedure for the Installation of a SQL*Plus client

Step 1: The installation of the SQL*Plus client is much like all other Oracle product client installations. Obtain the appropriate software media from Oracle Corp and install the software on the PC client. When the installation has completed correctly, proceed to Step 2.

Step 2: In order to use SQL*Plus, you must be able to connect to a known Oracle database at a known network address. All Oracle PC client products use the file TNSNAMES.ora to store their reference to the Oracle database servers to which they have access.

Locate the TNSNAMES.ora file on your PC under the general directory address: /ORACLE_HOME/network/admin. When you have located the file, you should open it to edit using a text editor like Notepad. Keep a backup copy of the original file in case the editing goes completely wrong.

Step 3: You will notice in the TNSNAMES.ora file that there are several connections or sample connections already defined. Each connection will have a general layout like this:

```
my_db =
 (DESCRIPTION =
  (ADDRESS_LIST =
   (ADDRESS  =  (PROTOCOL  =  TCP)(HOST  =
my_server)(PORT = 1521))
   )
  (CONNECT_DATA =
   (SERVICE_NAME = my_oracle_db)
   )

  )
```

Step 4: To create your own connection, copy and paste a sample connection and alter the following settings to suit your own environment:

> **my_db:** Create a unique connection name which you will use with SQL*Plus.

> **my_server:** Here use the IP address or network name of the server which hosts your Oracle instance.

> **my_oracle_db:** Here enter the name of the Oracle database service to which you wish to connect.

Step 5: When you think you have made a correct connection entry then save the edited TNSNAMES.ora file again (in its original location). You should now be able to connect to your chosen database using the connection information you have defined and with a valid username and password.

11.2 Troubleshooting a TNS client installation: Very often a TNS client installation like that used to install SQL*Plus on a PC fails to allow a connection to the database from the SQL*Plus client. Here are a few tips for troubleshooting the TNS connection:

> **Step 1:** Ping the host from your PC. Get a DOS prompt and get to drive C, then execute the following command:

> **C:> ping my_server**

> If you don't get a response or if you get this message:

> "Ping request could not find host my_server. Please check the name and try again."

> then your server name in the TNSNAME.ora file is wrong or is not recognised. Try using an IP address or call your network admin to get the correct server id.

> **Step 2:** If the ping in step 1 works and the SQL*Plus connection is still failing, try the following command:

> C:>tnsping **my_db**

> If you don't get a response or you get this message:

> "TNS-03505: Failed to resolve name",

> this indicates that either the value for **my_oracle_db**, the port number (e.g. 1521) or the network protocol (e.g. TCP) is incorrect. Check the TNS Listener port number and database

name with your DBA and the network protocol with your network admin.

11.3 SQL*Plus Client Interface: When the SQL*Plus client and DB connections are working, this is what a basic SQL*Plus client interface looks like:

```
Oracle SQL*Plus                                                    _|□|X|
File  Edit  Search  Options  Help

SQL*Plus: Release 10.1.0.4.2 - Production on Sat Jul 27 03:41:53 2013

Copyright (c) 1982, 2005, Oracle.  All rights reserved.


Connected to:
Oracle Database 10g Enterprise Edition Release 10.2.0.3.0 - Production
With the Partitioning, OLAP and Data Mining options

SQL> select * from scott.emp;

    EMPNO ENAME      JOB              MGR HIREDATE       SAL       COMM
---------- ---------- --------- ---------- --------- ---------- ----------
    DEPTNO
----------
      7369 SMITH      CLERK           7902 17-DEC-80       800
        20

      7499 ALLEN      SALESMAN        7698 20-FEB-81      1600        300
        30

      7521 WARD       SALESMAN        7698 22-FEB-81      1250        500
        30


    EMPNO ENAME      JOB              MGR HIREDATE       SAL       COMM
---------- ---------- --------- ---------- --------- ---------- ----------
    DEPTNO
```

11.4 Using the SQL*Plus Client: Notice the **SQL>** prompt above. This is where SQL commands are entered or PL/SQL statements are composed.

There are several in-built and useful commands available in SQL*Plus which can make working with the interface easier. This list isn't definitive but these are the most useful commands, accompanied by examples:

11.4.1 List last SQL statement: Use the 'l' command to show the last executed SQL statement:

>   SQL> l
>
>   1* select * from scott.emp
>
>   SQL>

11.4.2 Execute last statement: Use the '/' to execute the last entered SQL statement

SQL> /

...... select or insert, update, delete results....

11.4.3 Setting the SQL*Plus environment: The working environment of a SQL*Plus session can be set to alter the way data output is formatted and how the SQL*Plus environment appears.

This is done using either the GUI >Options>Environment or by using the SET command together with the appropriate parameter. For example, to set the terminal output ON, use the following command or set it in the GUI Options environment:

SQL> set termout ON

SQL>

11.4.4 Show All - displaying the current SQL*Plus environment: To see what the current environment settings are, use the "show all" command at the SQL prompt. There are many SQL*Plus environment settings. The following example shows just a few of these:

SQL> show all

appinfo is OFF and set to "SQL*Plus"

arraysize 15

autocommit OFF

autoprint OFF

autorecovery OFF

autotrace OFF

blockterminator "." (hex 2e)

btitle OFF and is the first few characters of the next SELECT stateme

cmdsep OFF

colsep " "

compatibility version NATIVE

concat "." (hex 2e)

copycommit 0

COPYTYPECHECK is ON

define "&" (hex 26)

describe DEPTH 1 LINENUM OFF INDENT ON

echo OFF

editfile "afiedt.buf"

embedded OFF

escape OFF

FEEDBACK ON for 6 or more rows

flagger OFF

flush ON

heading ON

headsep "|" (hex 7c)

11.4.4 Useful SQL*Plus parameter settings and commands: All SQL*Plus parameters are important, but some are more useful and worth remembering than others. These are a few that we find we use all the time:

- **Show:** Shows the value of a SQL*Plus system variable, or the current SQL*Plus environment. SHOW SGA requires a DBA privileged login.

- **Show user:** Show user is often useful when you are moving rapidly between many user ids or if you have many SQL sessions open at the same time. It can get confusing and at the SQL prompt, confusion can be very dangerous. "Show user" before executing an important command may allow a developer to confirm that they are executing against the correct database schema:

    SQL> show user

    USER is "OPMADMIN"

    SQL>

- **Show instance:** Show instance is often useful when you are moving rapidly between many database instances or if you have many SQL sessions open at the same time:

    SQL> show instance

    Instance "track"

    SQL>

- **SET Timing on:** Sets the timing on for a SQL statement execution. This can be useful for making very rough comparisons of SQL execution times, but remember that the time also includes terminal outputs, network traffic between server and client etc. so at the best it's a rough time only.

    14 rows selected.

82

Elapsed: 00:00:00.46

SQL>

- **Spooling outputs to a file:** Very often when testing a small tract of code, it is useful to send the output to a file and then look at the output in a text file, rather than looking at the results on screen. To do this, we first need to tell SQL to spool (send) the output to a file, then execute the command and then open the file with an editor to read the results. Here are the steps:

  Step 1: Spool an output file called mal.txt:

  SQL> spool mal.txt

  SQL>

  Step 2: Execute the SQL statement:

  SQL> select * from scott.emp;

  Step 3: Close the file:

  SQL> spool off

  Step 4: Open the file to read the contents in your text editor

  SQL> ed mal.txt

- **Debugging - Show errors:** When a PL/SQL error occurs, you can usefully display the full error by typing "show errors" at the SQL prompt as follows:

  SQL> show errors

  No errors.

- **Getting Help with the SET and SHOW commands:** Get basic help on the set commands as follows:

  SQL>help set

  SQL>help show

11.4.5 Editing and String substitution from the SQL prompt: You can use one of two handy utilities in SQL*Plus for editing SQL.

The first method allows a developer to invoke a text editor at any time whilst entering a SQL statement. The current statement is then displayed in the text editor. We can then continue editing the statement, save the statement and then execute it, using the "/" command or list it using the "l" command at the SQL prompt. To invoke the text editor (Notepad, in this case), type "ed" at the SQL prompt as follows:

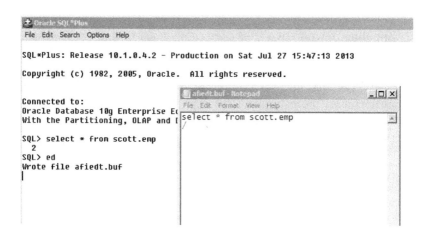

In the second case, a developer can carry out some primitive string substitutions at the SQL command line. For example, we could change "emp" to "employee" using the "c" string command as follows:

>select * from scott.emp

>SQL> c/emp/employees/

>select * from scott.employees

>SQL>

11.4.6 Describing a database table: Very often you may need to check the structure of a database table whilst at the SQL prompt. The easiest way to do this is to use the "desc" command, as in the following example, which returns the full table definition for the CUSTOMERS table.

>SQL>desc customers

11.4.7 The DUAL table: Very often in SQL it is logically necessary to select ONLY a single value, as in the case when we need to get the system date-time, for example. To do this we need a table that is guaranteed to only contain a single row. Oracle provides us with such a table and it is owned by the SYS super user but available to all users to select from. The name of this table is DUAL. Note that the record in this table cannot (in practise) be deleted or updated and no other records can be added to this table. It only ever contains a single record.

The next section will show some examples of when this table is useful. Note: If you do have SYS privilege in your database, do NOT be tempted to add a second record to dual or drop / truncate dual. This can have catastrophic effects throughout the database. DUAL is a data dictionary table and using SQL to modify such tables is NOT supported by Oracle.

11.4.8 SQL Pseudo-Columns: A pseudo-column is an Oracle assigned value used in the same context as an Oracle database column, but it is not stored in the database. SQL and PL/SQL recognize the following SQL pseudo-columns, which return specific data items: SYSDATE, SYSTIMESTAMP, ROWID, ROWNUM, UID, USER, LEVEL, CURRVAL, NEXTVAL, ORA_ROWSCN, etc.

Pseudo-Columns are not actual columns in a table but they behave like columns. For example, you can select values from a pseudo-column. However, you cannot insert into, update, or delete from a pseudo-column. Also note that pseudo-columns are allowed in SQL statements, but not in procedural statements. Here is a typical example of the syntax for using a pseudo-column:

SQL> SELECT sysdate, systimestamp FROM dual;

SYSDATE   SYSTIMESTAMP

--------- ---
12-DEC-09 12-DEC-09 10.02.31.956842 AM +02:00

Here are some brief explanations of some of the pseudo-columns available to the developer:

- **SYSDATE and SYSTIMESTAMP:** Return the current DATE and TIMESTAMP.

- **UID and USER:** Return the User ID and Name of a database user.

- **CURRVAL and NEXTVAL:** A sequence is a schema object that generates sequential numbers. When you create a sequence, you can specify its initial value and an increment. CURRVAL returns the current value in a specified sequence. Before you can reference CURRVAL in a session, you must use NEXTVAL to generate a number. A reference to NEXTVAL stores the current sequence number in CURRVAL. NEXTVAL increments the sequence and returns the next value. To obtain the current or next value in a sequence, you must use the dot notation, as follows:

  sequence_name.CURRVAL

sequence_name.NEXTVAL

- **ROWID** returns the rowid (binary address) of a row in a database table. You can use variables of type UROWID to store rowids in a readable format. Then you can compare the UROWID variable to the ROWID pseudo-column in the WHERE clause of a SELECT, UPDATE or DELETE statement to identify the latest row fetched from a cursor. A ROWID is the most efficient way of identifying a single record in a table.

- **ROWNUM** returns a number indicating the order in which a row was selected from a table. The first row selected has a ROWNUM of 1, the second row has a ROWNUM of 2, and so on. If a SELECT statement includes an ORDER BY clause, ROWNUMs are assigned to the retrieved rows before the sort is done. You can use ROWNUM in an UPDATE statement to assign unique values to each row in a table. Also, you can use ROWNUM in the WHERE clause of a SELECT statement to limit the number of rows retrieved (where rownum < 100 will only retrieve the first 100 records in a SELECT statement).

---o0o---

12. SQL - PL/SQL Development Tools

Writing PL/SQL is possible using the SQL*Plus interface. However, this is not an optimal way to work in a commercial development environment and generally PL/SQL developers tend to use a GUI-based development tool to assist in the task.

There are many Oracle and 3rd party tools available to aid the developer in designing, debugging, building and testing SQL and PL/SQL. TOAD is one of the best and most popular 3rd party tools available, and Oracle have recently released their own TOAD-like product called SQL Developer - which embodies many of the code development and database management features of TOAD.

We will now take a look at how SQL Developer can be useful. Many of the functions are so similar to TOAD that the reader should be able to easily transfer knowledge of one of these products when using the other.

12.1 The SQL Developer Interface: Here is SQL Developer being used to design and debug a PL/SQL Trigger:

12.2 SQL Developer Features. Here are the basic features of SQL Developer:

- Connection Browser: Browse database connections (Oracle and others)

- Schema Browser: Browse schema objects in a particular instance

- Schema Diff: Make comparisons between different schemas

- Create, alter, and drop all database objects

- Manage users and privileges

- Create and schedule database jobs

- Create and edit data models
- Manage database configuration
- Import and Export data to and from Oracle tables from various file formats

Specific Coding aids:

- PL/SQL debugger, Set Break Points
- Code Formatting assistant
- Debug Anonymous Blocks
- SQL Tuning Advisor
- Diff Tool for Explain Plans
- Query Builder
- SQL Worksheet - Build and execute SQL query
- SQL statement formatting
- Version control - Integration with CVS and Subversion
- SQL Developer provides a worksheet type interface.

---o0o---

13. Glossary of Terms.

3G language: Most popular general-purpose languages today such as C, C++, C#, Java, BASIC and Pascal, are also third-generation languages, although C++, Java and C# follow a completely different path, as they are object-oriented in nature.

Third generation (3G) languages tend to focus on software structures and structured development. They have no connection with concepts of object encapsulation, including the idea that a database table may autonomously incorporate its own validation rules, and may manifest and control its own behaviour under varying conditions, such as a database transaction.

APEX: Apex is Oracle Application Express, an Oracle product that has been a long time in development and is the latest in a set of Oracle front-end design and development tools. APEX is embedded and integrated into the application database and provides a sophisticated toolkit for rapid web application development against an Oracle database. APEX is basically a web front-end development environment, based on an Oracle database. For an experienced developer it can be a very good tool to produce a resilient dynamic html web-based front-end. Despite the claims of Oracle, it is really *not* a development tool for a novice. However, it is an excellent product and has rapidly replaced Oracle Forms and Reports as the front-end of choice for many Oracle applications where a web interface is needed.

API(s): Application Program Interface(s): An API specifies a set of functions or routines that accomplish a specific task, or allow an interaction with a specific software component. In PL/SQL an API is most generally built as a PL/SQL package which provides a complete standalone interface to a particular software function.

Constraints (database constraints): Constraints are rules of *data integrity* for a database that limit the acceptable data values for a table. They are the optional schema objects that depend on a table. The existence of a table without any constraint is possible, but the existence of a constraint without any table is not possible.

Constraints enforce business rules in a database. If a constraint is violated during a transaction, the transaction will fail, be rolled back and a specific error occurs.

Constraints can be created along with the table in the CREATE TABLE statement. Addition and deletion of constraints can be done in the ALTER TABLE statement. The following types of constraints are available in Oracle Database:

- **NOT NULL:** It enforces that a column, declared as not null, cannot have any NULL values. For example, if an employee's hire date is not known, then that employee may not be considered as a valid employee.

- **UNIQUE:** It ensures that columns protected by this constraint cannot have duplicate values.

- **PRIMARY KEY:** It is responsible for uniquely identifying a row in a table. A table can have only one PRIMARY KEY constraint. A PRIMARY KEY constraint wholly includes both the NOT NULL and UNIQUE constraints. It is enforced with an index on all columns in the key.

- **FOREIGN KEY:** It is also known as referential integrity constraint. It enforces that values referenced in one table, are defined in another table. It establishes a parent-child or reference-dependent relationship between the two tables.

- **CHECK:** It enforces that columns must meet a specific condition that is evaluated to a Boolean value. If the value evaluates to false, then the database will raise an exception and not allow the INSERT and UPDATE statements to operate on columns.

Data Consistency and Concurrency: In a single-user database, a user can modify data without concern for other users modifying the same data at the same time. However, in a multi-user database, statements within multiple simultaneous transactions can update the same data. Transactions executing simultaneously must produce meaningful and consistent results. Therefore, a multi-user database must provide the following conditions:

- Data concurrency, which ensures that users can access data at the same time.

- Data consistency, which ensures that each user sees a consistent view of the data, including visible changes made by the user's own transactions and committed transactions of other users.

To describe consistent transaction behaviour when transactions run concurrently, database researchers defined a "transaction isolation" model called serializability. A serializable transaction operates in an environment that makes it appear as if no other users were modifying data in the database.

While this isolation between transactions is generally desirable, running many applications in serializable mode can seriously compromise application throughput. Complete isolation of concurrently running transactions could mean that one transaction cannot perform an insertion into a table being queried by another transaction. So, basically, real-world considerations require a compromise between perfect transaction isolation and performance. Oracle maintains data consistency by using a so-called multi-version consistency model and various types of locks and transactions. In this way, the database can present a view of data to multiple concurrent users, with each view consistent to a point in time. Because different versions of data blocks can exist simultaneously, transactions can read the version of data committed at the point in time required by a query and return results that are consistent to a single point in time.

This complex infrastructure is built into Oracle Transaction Processing (TP) and developers need not concern themselves with it - it works very effectively.

Data Dictionary: Oracle's data dictionary provides information that Oracle needs in order to perform its tasks. This information consists of definitions, storage size for database objects (tables, views, indexes etc. etc.), default column values, integrity constraints, names of and privileges granted to users, auditing information and more. The data dictionary is stored in a group of tables owned by SYS (the so called dictionary base tables). Their content is available through static dictionary "views". These views and tables should not be written to, only selected. The base tables are stored in the SYSTEM tablespace - which is always available when the Oracle database is open.

DBA: A Database Administrator: This is the person (database "role") responsible for the installation, configuration, upgrade, administration, monitoring and maintenance of (Oracle) databases within an organisation or in a development project. The role includes the design and development of database strategies, database monitoring, database performance tuning and capacity planning for future expansion. A DBA is also responsible for the planning, co-ordination and implementation of security measures to safeguard controlled access to the database, database availability and database backup and failure management.

Edgar Codd (1923 - 2003) was an English computer scientist who, while working for IBM, invented the relational model for database management, the theoretical basis for relational databases. The relational model, a very influential general theory of data management, remains his most important achievement.

Indentation: In PL/SQL and SQL, as in much computer programming, an indentation style is a convention governing the indentation of blocks of software code to convey the program's structure. Indentation is not a requirement of PL/SQL or SQL. However, it does greatly increase the readability of a module of software. Various styles of indentation exist but basically it comes down to the appropriate indentation being used to indicate nesting of conditions, loops etc. The greater the nesting, the more indentation is used.

Index: An Index is an Oracle database object associated with a table. Indexes provide improved access to table rows by storing sorted values from specific columns and using those sorted values to find associated table rows more easily.

This means that data can be found without having to look at more than a fraction of the total rows within a table. Indexes are optional, but generally associated with primary and unique keys and often with foreign key columns. The use of indexes is not always positive. An index may improve data retrieval speed, but inserting data is less efficient, because every new record means that one or more indexes need to be updated. This reduces performance, which can be a disadvantage for OLTP database processing. However, in a data warehouse environment (where transaction processing doesn't happen), indexes can be used without too much consideration and generally yield performance improvements.

Instance (Oracle instance): A database instance is a set of memory structures that manage database files. A database is a set of physical files on disk, created by the "CREATE DATABASE" statement. The instance manages its associated data and serves the users of the database. Every running Oracle database is associated with at least one Oracle database instance.

Locking: In a multi-user system, many users may wish to update the same data at the same time. Locking allows only one user to update a particular data block, during which time another person cannot modify the same data. The basic idea of locking is, that when a user modifies data through a transaction, that data is locked by that transaction until the transaction is committed or rolled back. The lock is held until the transaction is complete: this is known as data concurrency,

The second purpose of locking is to ensure that all processes have read access to the original data as they were at the time the query began (modification not yet committed). This is known as read consistency.

Although locks are vital to enforce database consistency, they can create performance problems. Every time one process issues a lock, another user may be shut out from updating/deleting the locked row or table. Oracle allows a user to lock whatever resources they need. This can be a single row, many rows, an entire table, and even many tables. But the larger the scope of the lock, the more processes are potentially shut out to processing by other users. However, data can always be viewed by other users in its pre-committed state.

Non-unique index: You can use Non-unique indexes to improve the performance of data access, when the values of the columns in the index are not necessarily unique.

Advice: Do not create Non-unique indexes on very small tables, because scans of small tables alone are usually more efficient than using an index and then also accessing the table.

Object-Relational database: An object-relational database (ORD), or object-relational database management system (ORDBMS), is a database management system (DBMS) similar to a relational database but, with an object-oriented database model, objects, classes and inheritance are directly supported in database schemas and in the query language. In addition, just as with proper relational systems, it supports extension of the data model with custom data-types and methods. Oracle can be used as an Object-Relational database.

An Object-Relational database can be said to provide a middle ground between relational databases and object-oriented databases (OODBMS). In object-relational databases, the approach is essentially that of relational databases: the data resides in the database and is manipulated collectively with queries in a query language; at the other extreme are OODBMS, in which the database is essentially a persistent object store for software written in an object-oriented programming language, with a programming API for storing and retrieving objects, and little or no specific support for querying.

OLAP: On-line Analytical Processing: This is a type or part of a system, characterized by a relatively low volume of transactions but with very many and very profound queries. Queries are often very complex and involve complex data aggregations. For OLAP systems, a response time is a measure of effectiveness. OLAP applications are widely used by Data Mining techniques. In an OLAP database there is aggregated, historical data, stored in multi-dimensional schemas (usually star schema) which may be heavily denormalized.

OLTP: On-line Transaction processing: This is a type or part of a system which is characterized by a large number of short on-line transactions (INSERT, UPDATE, and DELETE). The main emphasis for OLTP systems is put on very fast query processing, maintaining data integrity in multi-access environments and an effectiveness measured by the number of transactions per second. OLTP is the "system opposite" of OLAP (On-line Analytical Processing), which is used to aggregate and obtain information rather than make user transactions.

Oracle Developer Suite: In the latest release, Oracle Developer Suite consists of the following components:

- **Oracle Forms:** Oracle Forms is a software product for creating screens that interact with an Oracle database. It has an IDE including an object navigator, property sheet and code editor that uses PL/SQL. It was originally developed to run server-side in character mode terminal sessions. It was ported to other platforms, including Windows, to function in a client-server environment. Later versions were ported to Java, where it runs in a Java EE container and can integrate with Java and web services. The primary focus of Forms is to create data entry systems that access an Oracle database. Oracle Forms is integrated into Oracle Designer, and Forms can be generated directly from the Module Design toolset.

- **Oracle Reports:** Oracle Reports is a tool for developing reports against data stored in an Oracle database. Oracle Reports consists of Oracle Reports Developer and Oracle Application Server Reports Services (a component of the Oracle Application Server). Oracle Reports is integrated into Oracle Designer, and Reports can be generated directly from the Module Design toolset.

- **Oracle Designer:** Oracle's primary CASE tool (as of 10g). Useful for Analysis, Logical and Physical design, process modelling, schema modelling and functional and module design and build.

- **Oracle Discoverer:** Oracle Discoverer is a tool-set for ad-hoc querying, reporting, data analysis, and Web-publishing for the

Oracle Database environment. Oracle Corporation markets it as a business intelligence product. It was originally a stand-alone product. However, it has become a component of the Oracle Fusion Middleware suite, and was renamed Oracle Business Intelligence Discoverer.

- **Oracle JDeveloper:** JDeveloper is a freeware IDE supplied by Oracle Corporation. It offers features for development in Java, XML, SQL and PL/SQL, HTML, JavaScript, BPEL and PHP. JDeveloper covers the full development lifecycle from design through to coding, debugging, optimisation and profiling to deploying.

Performance: Oracle performance is usually measured by processing cycle times, or data throughput rates. Oracle performance can be a critical issue in very large databases (VLDB), where mission-critical tasks can be delayed by poor processing times. Also, performance is not a static issue. Performance may degrade over time as data volumes or the number of user processes increase, or as tables or indexes become more and more disorganised. Performance is generally affected by the following issues: Appropriate server sizing, careful Oracle instance configuration, optimal physical database design (indexes, partitioning etc), SQL software design (optimal access path for retrieving data), and the quality and frequency of database maintenance.

PL/SQL: Procedural Language/Structured Query Language (PL/SQL) is Oracle's procedural extension language for SQL and the Oracle database. SQL is limited by not having any procedure syntax. The concept of "if" simply doesn't exist in SQL. SQL is a set language and deals only with the basic transactional events of INSERT, UPDATE, and DELETE, and of course, the basic query syntax of SELECT.

Prior to PL/SQL, programmers were obliged to "wrap up" tracts of SQL in other 3G languages (which Oracle provided) such as Pro*C, Pro*Cobol, etc. Whilst this worked fine, Oracle needed a new procedural language which could be stored and executed from within the database itself, and PL/SQL was therefore released with Oracle version 7. It has a full set of procedural syntax and is a relatively easy language to use. Needless to say, the PL/SQL is very much biased towards database processing and has a limited amount of other non-dataset I/O facilities.

Primary and unique keys - the differences: In logical database design, a normalised entity is allocated a Unique Identifier (UID). This UID consists of one or more attributes which, taken together, can be used to uniquely identify one instance of that entity (or one record in a table).

For example, in a Human Resources database this unique identifier might be Social Security Number or some artificial "surrogate" key created by the company, such as Employee Id. Very often an entity has more than one possible unique identifier. Name, date of birth and place of birth can perhaps be used as a unique id in some applications. During the transition from logical design to physical design, certain decisions need to be made about these identifiers. One of them must be selected as the Primary Key of the table, and the remaining alternative unique identifiers must be defined as unique keys. A primary key is the main method by which a record is identified. Unique keys are alternate methods of identifying a record. Both types of key MUST be unique, and the database will enforce this uniqueness using Primary and Unique Key Constraints, which basically enforce the uniqueness using Unique Indexes on the defined columns. It is therefore imperative to be absolutely sure about the definition of these keys during the Oracle database design phase.

Procedures and Triggers: PL/SQL program units can be stored as procedures and triggers in the database. This is a very useful way of controlling the behaviour of a table during a DML transaction. For example, imagine that an Order Header table also stores the total value for all its Order Lines as a denormalized column. When a new order line is added, this total must be recalculated and the Order Header table updated. The same is true when an Order line is deleted or updated. Again, the order header total value needs to be recalculated and the Order Header table kept up-to-date with the new total value.

- This scenario is ideally managed using 3 triggers on the Order Line table which will "fire" ON-INSERT, ON-UPDATE, and ON-DELETE.

- Each of these triggers then calls a stored PL/SQL procedure, called, for example, RECALCULATE_ORDER_TOTAL.

- This procedure will recalculate the sum of the ORDER_LINE_VALUE and then issue an UPDATE of the ORDER_HEADER table to update the stored total value.

Rollback: Use the ROLLBACK statement to undo work done in the current transaction, or to manually undo the work done by an in-doubt distributed transaction. If a transaction or set of transactions has been done on a set of table data, it can be reverted in the same session using the ROLLBACK command. Rollback is the transactional opposite to COMMIT.

Row-level locking: When an UPDATE statement is issued that affects a group of rows in a table: all of the affected rows are locked immediately. Of course, other processes continue to be able to read any row in the table, including the ones that are actually being updated. When other processes do read updated rows, they see only the old version of the row prior to update (via a rollback segment), until the changes are actually *committed*. This is known as a consistent read. The row-level locks are held until the locking process issues either a COMMIT or ROLLBACK statement.

With row-level locking, each row within a table can be locked individually. Locked rows can be updated only by the locking process. All other rows in the table are still available for updating by other processes.

Schema: A schema is the set of objects (tables, views, indexes, etc) that belong to a user account. The word is also often used as another way to refer to an Oracle user.

Schema Diff: The management of change in a database system can be complex and needs careful management as part of an overall Version Control strategy. One important aspect of this is quality assurance of change implementation in databases. For example, a change request may generate several database changes which are then made and implemented in a single release. In order to guarantee that database schema changes have been correctly and fully implemented, it is very useful to compare a "Before" and "After" view of a changed database schema. There are many tools which can be used to do this, including SQL Developer and TOAD. The process of comparing the 2 schemas is often called "Diffing", i.e. "finding the Differences". The output from the process is called a Schema Diff and shows only the differences between the 2 schemas in an ordered report.

Security: data and functional: Oracle provides very granular and very safe built-in security functions which operate at a role, user, privilege, object, row, and column level.

- **Basic User Functional Privileges:** When a user account is created, they are allocated certain group privileges. A normal operational user would be allocated so-called CONNECT privileges. This would not allow them to create private database objects such as tables, but would allow them to connect to the database as a basic user. A developer would be granted RESOURCE privilege, which allows them to use DML commands, and a DBA would receive DBA privilege, which gives them the right to create database objects and grant privileges on them to others, etc.

- **Roles and Tables:** When tables have been created as part of a database build, they are only accessible to the application owner/user and the DBA. No-one else has any form of access to these tables. They must first be granted explicit access to these tables to perform the explicit operations SELECT, INSERT, UPDATE, DELETE.

  So, in addition to granting users these basic roles, a database administrator and the application designer would also define and create a matrix of user roles into which all physical users would fall. For example, a role of "Invoice Entry" would:

  GRANT SELECT, INSERT, UPDATE, DELETE

  on invoice_headers to invoice_entry_role"

  "GRANT SELECT, INSERT, UPDATE, DELETE

  on invoice_lines to invoice_entry_role"

- **Roles and Users:** Any new user joining the Invoice entry team would then be granted this role and thus inherit its privileges as follows:

  "GRANT INVOICE_ENTRY_ROLE to NEW_USER"

  The effect of this would be that this user would have the right to insert, update, delete and select from the INVOICE_HEADERS and INVOICE_LINES tables.

- **Restricting Data access:** A user or role can be explicitly excluded from any or all forms of access to a particular dataset within a table, using various methods, including database views or the use of Virtual Private Database (VPD). This enables you to create security policies to control database access at the row and column level. Essentially, Oracle Virtual Private Database adds a dynamic WHERE clause to a SQL statement that is issued against the table, view, or synonym to which an Oracle Virtual Private Database security policy was applied.

From these simple examples we can see that Oracle provides an extremely safe and very granular level of security. The whole subject of security is an important component in application design, and the priority is to design a simple but resilient method of administrating users, which guarantees data and functional security.

SQL Optimiser: In Oracle the SQL Optimiser attempts to determine the most efficient way to execute a given query by considering the possible query plans. When SQL queries are submitted to the database server, they are first parsed to ensure they are syntactically correct and refer to real database objects, and they are then passed to the query optimiser where the query execution is planned and optimised.

The optimiser works out the most efficient data access path (the so-called Execution Plan) based on many factors such as the existence of Indexes, the structure of the SQL, the size of the tables involved etc. The optimiser's decisions can be influenced by using SQL Hints in the code, by adding and changing database structures, and by improving SQL coding strategies. The optimiser produces the best execution plan in the circumstances. However, this may still give rise to a very poor performance. Very often human judgement and design changes are required to actually improve performance.

Unique Index: Unique indexes are used to ensure that no identical key values are stored in a table. When we create a table that contains a primary key, we must also create a unique index for that table on the primary key. Unique indexes are also created on other unique keys defined for a table.

Unit and System Testing: There are several levels of software testing. Unit testing and System testing are 2 important components of a complete test regime. Other testing components may include Integration testing, Load testing, Scalability testing etc.

- **Unit testing**, also known as component testing refers to tests that verify the functionality of a specific section of code, usually at a functional level. These types of tests are usually written by developers as they work on code to ensure that the specific function is working as expected. Unit testing alone cannot verify the functionality of a piece of software, but rather is used to assure that the building blocks the software uses work independently of each other.

- **System Testing:** System testing of software is conducted on a complete, integrated system to evaluate the system's compliance with its specified requirements. System testing falls within the scope of black box testing, and as such, should require no knowledge of the inner design of the code or logic. As a rule, system testing takes, as its input, all of the "integrated" software components that have successfully passed integration testing and also the software system itself. The purpose of integration testing is to detect any inconsistencies between the software units that are integrated together or between any of the assemblages and the hardware. System testing is a more limited type of testing; it seeks to detect defects within the system as a whole.

  System testing is performed on the entire system in the context of a Functional Requirement Specification and a System Requirement Specification. System testing tests not only the design, but also the behaviour, and even the expectations of the customer. It is also intended to test up to and beyond the bounds defined in the software/hardware requirements specification.

Version Control: In this context, version control refers to the management of changes to software programs. Changes are usually identified by a number or letter code, termed a "revision number" or "revision level". For example, an initial set of software files may be defined as "revision 1". When the first change is made, the resulting set is called "revision 2", and so on. Each revision is associated with a timestamp and the persons making the changes. Revisions can be compared, restored, and with some types of files, merged. These days, version control is vital to the management of software development and maintenance, and most commercial developments use version control software systems to manage change to modules, databases and entire software applications.

---o0o---

About the Author

Malcolm Coxall, the author, is a business and IT systems analyst and consultant with more than 30 years freelance experience in Europe and the Middle East. Malcolm has worked in Oracle systems design and development for the last 25 years as a developer, business analyst, database designer, DBA, systems administrator, team lead and project manager.

With experience working for many of the world's largest corporate and institutional players, as well as for several government and international agencies, Malcolm has extensive hands-on experience in designing and building large-scale Oracle systems in many diverse vertical markets such as banking, oil, defence, telecoms, manufacturing, mining, food, agriculture, aerospace, and engineering.

Malcolm also writes and publishes books, papers and articles on human system design, sociology, environmental economics, sustainable technology and technology in environmental protection and food production.

Malcolm lives in southern Spain from where he continues his freelance Oracle consultancy and his writing, whilst managing the family's organic farm.

---o0o---